Eternal as a Weed

Tales of Ozark Experience from Creative Writing of Columbia

Bridget Bufford, Editor

Photography by Yolanda Ciolli used with permission.

Published by Compass Flower Press
Columbia, Missouri

ISBN 978-1-942168-63-8

Contents

Introduction

I know I am handsome and young and drunk
eternal as a weed

From *The Forgotten Madmen of Ménilmontant,*
Frank Stanford, 1948 - 1978

A year ago, I remarked in my workshop that I hear such great writing in our weekly meetings; it's a shame that little of the work gets a wider audience. I've always thought we should put together a reading, or maybe an anthology, but thinking about the possibilities never brought them to fruition. Workshop members Rebecca Graves, Sady Mayer Strand, and Von Pittman all liked the idea of a collection. The very soul of our connection developed from writing to prompts, so we agreed that a theme was necessary.

Why Ozarks? It's a part of Missouri rich in associations. I think of caves, sinkholes and springs; catalpa, black walnut, shagbark hickory and persimmons. Sassafras, witch hazel, sumac, greenbrier and poison ivy. For someone of a less botanical bent, the Ozarks might evoke a trip to Silver Dollar City, a Mason jar of moonshine or a jet ski at the Lake. Several Creative Writing of Columbia members have lived in the Ozarks, and nearly all of us have been there.

I put out a call for submissions from current and former members of Creative Writing of Columbia: poetry, fiction or essays that touched upon the selected theme. The responses were wonderful—mostly new work, plus some old favorites from so many of the writers I've enjoyed throughout the years.

Yolanda Ciolli of AKA-Publishing and Compass Flower Press offered her wisdom and inspiration throughout the process. Thanks to Yolanda, Von, Sady, and Rebecca for their encouragement; to the anonymous donor who helped make this happen; and to all the writers included herein.

Above all, I want to thank my mentor Pat Schneider, Ozark native and founder of Amherst Writers & Artists, for her wise and instructive presence along the way.

Acknowledgements

Grateful acknowledgment is made for the permission to reprint the following works:

"Saying Goodbye to an Ozark Original" by Tracy Barnett first appeared in:
http://tracybarnettonline.com/blog/2010/04/14/saying-goodbye-to-an-ozark-original/#more-1076

"Earl's Barn" by Jim Coffman first appeared in *Interpretations III* (Columbia, MO: Columbia Art League, 2015).

"Winter" by Kathleen Cain first appeared in *Interpretations IV* (Columbia, MO: Columbia Art League, 2016).

"1,000 Miles" by Bridget Bufford first appeared in the *Harrington Lesbian Fiction Quarterly* (Volume 3:2, 2002).

A Talk with a Stranger

Von Pittman

I fell in with a bunch of self-anointed pseudo-bohemians during my junior year at Drury. Back in 1963 all it took to be a rebel in Springfield was to stay up late at night and to talk occasionally about foreign films. Most nights at around one-thirty or two, a group of us walked to one of three nearby all-night restaurants. One February night only Alan and I faced the cold, heading to Eddie's for French toast. One notch above a greasy spoon, Eddie's featured a strong, molasses-flavored syrup. Hank Williams dominated its jukebox. At 2:30 a.m., almost nobody was there. Three night-men from the *Springfield News-Leader* were taking their dinner break. An old man sat in a booth, sipping coffee and staring at a spot a thousand miles away. He took out his last Pall Mall, lit up, then crumpled the empty pack.

He wore a pair of threadbare navy blue slacks, a denim shirt with a bolo tie, and a wrinkled black jacket. His scuffed spectator wingtips were not a good match for his outfit or the gray fedora pushed onto the back of his head. A small straw and cardboard suitcase, with fake leather trim, sat beside him.

"What do you suppose his story is?" Alan said.

"Just a traveling man, down on his luck," I said. "He and his elegant luggage will be on the next Greyhound." Given that the bus station was less than two blocks down from Eddie's, that seemed about right.

"Wonder why he came through here?"

"Must be on his way to St. Louis."

Betty came and took our French toast orders. "Let's buy him a cup of coffee and see if he'll tell us his story," Alan said. If you bought a meal at Eddie's, Johnny, the night manager, would let the waitresses serve you as many coffee refills as you wanted. But if you came in and ordered only coffee, one cup was your limit. The old man was obviously resigned to this practice. He sipped infrequently and slowly. Alan went over to his booth and invited him to join us. Then he signaled Betty for more coffee. She looked toward Johnny, who gave a cursory nod. We were good customers. She poured a refill for the old man.

He said, "Appreciate it."

"Just passing through our fair city tonight?"

The man stared at his cup, probably wondering whether a refill was worth having to talk with two smartasses. I took a nearly full pack of Raleighs out of my jacket and offered him one. He took it, then tore the filter off. He pulled out a box of wooden matches and lit up. After a long drag, he said, "Thanks, partner."

We waited him out. Finally he said, "Just did a show out in Carthage, out at the VFW post."

Alan took one of my Raleighs and lighted it with his Zippo. "You're in show business, then?"

The man placed his matchbox on the table. Using two fingers, he began to slowly push it around. He pushed it about three inches, up and down, left and right, in circles, all very slowly. Then it was gone! It was not as if the box disappeared. Rather, it suddenly ceased to *be*. We didn't know when it had gone away, and we sure as Hell didn't have any idea where.

"You're a magician!" I said.

"Good for you, Sherlock," he said. Then, suddenly, the matchbox appeared, spinning in the exact center of the Formica tabletop, at least a foot from each of his hands.

"What's your stage name?" Alan said.

The old man took another of my Raleighs. "Saving up ten thousand coupons so you can get an ice bucket or a set of barbecue grill tools?" The Brown and Williamson Tobacco Company used to attach a coupon to each pack of Raleighs, and four bonus coupons to each carton. Like S&H Green Stamps, customers could then trade the coupons for assorted items of merchandise.

"Since I spend money on cigarettes, I might as well get some of it back," I said.

The man rubbed his thumb across a lapel pin. Obviously cheap, it was black, with some of the enamel rubbed off. A plain capital "B" appeared in the center. "You didn't tell us your stage name," Alan said.

The magician pointed at the lapel pin, but said nothing. He held out his cup when Betty came by.

"Are you one of the Blackstones?" I said.

"Harry Senior's nearly eighty, but he's still performing out in Hollywood. Harry Junior's already doing big shows in Las Vegas. He's been on Ed Sullivan," said our entertainer.

"Are you a cousin or brother, or something?" I asked.

The man again touched the lapel pin with his thumb and winked. A worn pack of cards appeared out of nowhere. The man slid the deck in front of Alan and said, "Cut." At about the same time, he took another of my Raleighs, tore the filter off, and lit up. He shuffled, spread the deck and told me to pick a card—but not to let Alan or him see it—then slide it back into the deck. I did as he directed. Jack of Spades. He shuffled again, and again told Alan to cut. He told me to slide a card out of the deck, then to leave it face down. I did.

"What card did you select on the first shuffle?"

"Jack of Spades," I said.

"Turn your new card over."

I flipped the card. A Raleigh cigarette coupon was stuck over the card's face. After taking in our slack jaws for a few seconds, he peeled the coupon off to reveal the Jack of Spades.

"How the *Hell* did you do that?" Alan almost shouted.

The man stood up and pulled his fedora forward, brim over his eyes. "Bus leaves for St. Louis in ten minutes. Much obliged for the coffee." He picked up his suitcase, then opened the front door and turned right, headed toward the bus station.

"He never did say whether he was a Blackstone, or even a professional magician," Alan said. "We either met a poor relation from one of the most accomplished families in magic, or the most skilled grifter I've ever run into." Alan liked to use words like "grifter."

"Whoever he was, he left with my pack of cigarettes," I said.

Two nights later, Alan and I, and two other aspiring hipsters, were at Eddie's eating French toast and listening to Hank Williams crooning "Lovesick Blues." Alan spoke up. "I called the Carthage VFW. They don't hire entertainers. They haven't booked an act in there since the Korean War. We were conned."

"So what?" I said. "It was the cheapest con we'll ever run into. That old man was the best sleight-of-hand artist I've ever seen. And the price was right—a cup of coffee and a pack of cigarettes. Less than a buck altogether. That's not too bad a loss to a down-on-his-luck grifter. And how the Hell did he stick that Raleigh coupon onto the Jack of Spades? I'm smoking Marlboros from now on."

Barnstormers' Trajectory

Von Pittman

"Bobbie, you better put out that cigarette before Donna catches you."

"Yeah, like Donna doesn't smoke like a chimney," Bobbie said. She dropped her third Kent of the day onto the pavement and ground it out with her right Spalding Oxford. "I wish she'd come on. We need to get on to Bentonville. We need some solid practice before tonight's game."

"Damn straight," said Charlene. "Our ball handling has been sloppy for the last couple of weeks. Our shooting's been worse. If we hadn't been playing such bad teams, we'd have lost a couple of games."

"And our hair was worse than our ball handling," said Bobbie. "We probably need to double the hair spray. I heard Donna say she was going to start buying six cases of Aqua Net at a time."

"Welcome to barnstorming, Bobbi—set shots, sloppy passing, and stiff, scratchy hair."

Charlene and Bobbi were the leading scorers on the Rolla Rockets, a touring women's team formed in imitation of the All American Redheads. The Redheads had started out in Cassville, Missouri, in 1936, and now played all over the country. As of 1967, four years into their team's lifespan, the Rockets still played all of their games in the Ozarks, or in towns within a day's drive.

The Rockets—like the Redheads—played according to men's rules, competing against pickup teams of police, teachers, lawyers, as well as church- and town-league teams. A share of the gate always went to a local charity.

All the female barnstorming teams had a gimmick, invariably related to hair. The Redheads took the court with garish red-dyed bouffant hairstyles. The Rolla Rockets wore "beehive" hairdos. The action of fast—and often rough—games demanded amazing quantities of hair spray to keep their hair standing tall. Once, after purchasing three cases of Aqua Net, Donna had said, "What the Redheads are to henna, the Rockets are to Aqua Net! I swear, I wish I owned a whole bunch of Aqua Net stock."

Donna came out of the café and unlocked the team's 1957 Chevrolet panel truck. Charlene yelled "shotgun," and ran to the passenger door. Donna turned over the engine that her husband—and team co-owner—Mel kept running like silk. "The other girls are at the beauty shop. Thelma and her assistant are teasing out the last two right now. We should get to Bentonville around three. You girls could use some practice. We want 1967 to be our best year. A good game on Tuesday means a better gate on Wednesday and Thursday."

"You say that every night, Donna."

"It's true every night, Char."

When Donna pulled onto the highway, Charlene said, "We need to talk a little bit. Our pay was twenty-five dollars short last week. And it's impossible to eat three meals a day on two dollars and seventy-five cents. Can't you tell Mel to raise our meal allowance to about three-and-a-quarter, and to give us the twenty-five dollars you owe us?"

Donna sighed and assumed her familiar long-suffering look. "You know our crowds have been a little down lately. We're playing in some hick towns we never should have booked. But that's done. In a couple of weeks we'll be playing in Springfield, Osage Beach, and Fulton—places that have always done well for us."

Charlene wasn't ready to let go. "We've been working our butts off for you and Mel and you aren't paying us squat!"

"Char, Honey, the gates just haven't been as good this year. Last night in Hollister, we only sold 250 adult tickets. Last year we drew 325 there. There have been too many nights like that."

Bobbie chimed in. "How could we not be covering the overhead? With two hundred and fifty tickets at two-seventy-five, that should come close to seven hundred dollars."

"Six hundred eighty-seven dollars and fifty cents, Bobbie," said Donna. "But a hundred and fifty went to the hospital board. The high school charged us seventy-five dollars for their gym and locker rooms and fifteen bucks for paying the janitor to sweep and lock up. And that is before paying all of you, and your food and rooms. And don't forget the beauty shops and hair spray. I swear I'm gonna buy some Aqua Net stock."

Thelma's Chat and Curl stood on the edge of town. Donna pulled to the curb and the other members of the team—Sharon the 5'10" center, Robin, Nancy, and Mary Beth—came out holding makeup cases and small overnight bags. They arranged themselves on the two rows of bench seats and a single jump seat that Mel had bolted in for Sharon. Besides being the tallest of the Rockets, Sharon was the most striking. Her amazing ash-blonde beehive and sharply angled Star Trek-style eyebrows made her look even taller. She said, "Donna, when are you going to get a decent car for us to ride in? I hear the Redheads have custom-fitted Oldsmobile station wagons."

"How do you think we'd fit your hair into an Olds, Honey? You are the main reason we need a truck." It wasn't true, but it always worked when Sharon started bitching about the team truck.

Donna was used to complaints. The girls knew the Rockets didn't draw like the Redheads, and never would. She also knew that none of them had any particular skills beyond basketball. None had graduated from college. Hell, none of them had ever even been admitted to college. None could type. Not one even held a cosmetology license. All knew they would have to take a cut in income when they left barnstorming.

"Who are we playing tonight?" Robin said.

"The Bentonville Police Department. They'll probably have a few county sheriff's deputies, and maybe a game warden or two," Donna said.

Charlene stopped looking for a Top 40 station on the radio. "Some cops are in pretty good shape."

"Most aren't," said Donna.

Charlene said, "We were slow on the breaks and backdoor cuts last week. I'll bet all our shooting averages were off. Mine was."

Charlene, a guard, was both fast and quick, a deadeye shot, and a perfectionist. She had always wanted to be a professional athlete. In high school, she played basketball and ran sprints and relays on the girls' track team. She learned early that few women were making a living in professional sports. A handful of golfers and "amateur" tennis players taking money under the table were about it. There were no women's professional basketball leagues.

Then the All American Redheads came to town. They played according to men's rules, but put together a faster, flashier product, based on superior ball handling and shooting skills, coordination, teamwork, and conditioning. The Redheads easily outplayed the best men's team in town, the Church League Champion First Baptist Church. Entranced, Charlene suddenly had a goal.

The Redheads, and imitators like the Ozark Hillbillies and the Rolla Rockets, played wherever they could find audiences. This tended to be in small towns with little competition for the entertainment dollar. Most barnstorming teams won about eighty percent of their games, playing taller and stronger—but less well conditioned and practiced—men's teams.

The barnstorming team owners recruited the best high school and Amateur Athletic Union (AAU) team players they could find. In her junior year, Charlene attended a Redheads open tryout, even though she had not reached the minimum age to sign a contract. Her shooting and passing impressed the coaches, but the slower girls' game had not equipped her with the quick reflexes and stamina essential for the Redheads.

During her senior year, Charlene's high school coach started training her for stamina and agility. When the Rockets scheduled an open tryout in Rolla, Charlene caught a bus. She was exactly the kind of player Donna and Mel wanted. An excellent outside shooter, she made perfect passes to the other guard on backdoor cuts for easy layups. Mel and Donna gave her a one-year contract. The pay was poor and the travel awful. *But it's a shot. I won't have to be a waitress.*

In her first two years with the Rockets, Charlene improved every facet of her game. She hoped for another look from the Redheads. It didn't get any better for female athletes. She could either step up to the Redheads and make decent money, or end up as a night-shift waitress at White's Truck Stop.

Bentonville High School turned over its gym floor to the Rockets at 4 p.m., just as the last P.E. class finished up. The team ran through all its drills crisply and enthusiastically. Donna yelled, "Robin, Mary Beth, be sure to stretch your hamstrings well, now and at the end of practice." She hated injuries. The Rockets couldn't afford them. They travelled with only six players. One substitute, usually Nancy, had the job of giving all the starters about ten minutes' rest per half. If only five players were healthy enough to play, then Donna had to suit up and play the substitute's role. While she could still dribble and pass, her shooting eye was gone. So was her endurance. She was within shouting distance of forty, and had smoked close to two packs of Salems per day for nearly ten years. She wanted to keep her playing days behind her.

In the locker room, after a quick round of Coca-Colas and crackers, they got into their shiny red one-piece, snap-front game uniforms. Then they went to work on each other's hair, retouching the damage from practice and thoroughly fogging the locker room with Aqua Net. "You girls looked like a real team," said Donna. "That's what we've been missing for the last couple of weeks. These cops are not going to know what hit 'em."

Their sacrificial opponents, the "Bentonville Lawmen," had borrowed blue cotton gym shorts from the High School's P.E. department. They wore white strap undershirts with numbers drawn on in black marker. They nervously kidded each other as they set up lines for lay-up drills, then took random jump shots. A few looked relatively athletic, but most carried extra pounds around their waistlines. The few night shift patrolmen and jailers looked pale, even pasty. The day shift officers had finely tanned left arms.

Like all barnstorming basketball teams—male or female—the Rockets always started their show with a warm-up circle. The Harlem Globetrotters had introduced this feature back in the 1920s, making a series of intricate trick passes to a recording of "Sweet Georgia Brown." The Rockets had developed a unique drill. They could not match the showmanship of the Globetrotters; they compensated with speed, performing to the frantic pace of "Wipeout," by the Ventures. In the last minute of the routine, the six of them moved three balls at top speed simultaneously, which never failed to energize the crowd for the tipoff.

The Lawmen's center easily beat Sharon on the tipoff. But Charlene instantly batted the loose ball to Robin. Mary Beth had broken for the Rockets' basket at the tip. Robin led her perfectly with a long, two-handed pass. Mary Beth caught it in stride and scored on an easy layup. The crowd yelled and clapped. Few had ever seen girls or women play the full-court game, much less throw a half-court pass.

The Lawmen tentatively moved the ball toward the half-court line. Bobbie darted in on a diagonal line, stole the ball from a bewildered guard, then drove unimpeded to the basket and raised the score to 4-0. Once again the police brought the ball up carefully. A guard threw a high pass to their center. He hurried his shot and threw up an air ball. The Rockets recovered it and swiftly advanced the ball the length of the court on a series of quick, sharp passes, with no dribbling at all. The police team sagged back to defend their basket, so Charlene threw up a set shot from three feet outside the top of the key. In under a minute the Rockets were up 6-0.

The Rockets played according their standard game plan, which called for them to run up the score in the first quarter and to use the second quarter to show off trick shots and passes. During the half, they chugged down another Coke and added about another quarter-can each of Aqua Net to their beehives. The third quarter centered on gags and comedy bits. In the fourth, they returned to running up the score.

By the middle of the final quarter all sense of competition was gone. The home town Lawmen were winded. A couple of them started taking subtle cheap shots at the Rockets. This kind of reaction was not unusual. The women spread out and went into a stall, so that any blows would be blatantly obvious. They took only outside shots. On defense, the Rockets sagged back, encouraging their opponents to put up shots. They had the score well in hand, so a few more police points didn't matter. By then, those in the audience who weren't thinking about getting their kids to bed were anticipating a quick beer or two.

Everybody was ready for the final horn. They gave the Rockets an enthusiastic—but quick—standing ovation, then filed out. The Rockets and the cops lined up for perfunctory handshakes and the announcer thanked everyone for attending. The Rockets slipped on their cotton sweatpants and red nylon logo jackets and filed straight through the locker room to the parking lot, where Donna already had the truck running. "Great game tonight!" she said. "Good gate."

“We could have beaten the Redheads tonight,” Charlene said. “Damn, we looked good! Donna, you had better get serious and get us our back pay and up our meal allowance.”

Donna didn’t answer. But she stopped at a Texaco station and bought two six-packs of Busch Bavarian and a bag of ice. “As soon as we get back, get your showers. Team meeting in my room in thirty minutes.” After letting the players out, she drove around to the motel office and picked up the outdoor pay phone.

The players, who bunked three to a room, and had to take turns in the showers, rushed to get to Donna’s room at the allotted time. Charlene led the way. “Donna said it was a good gate. Maybe we’re gonna get a bonus, or at least our back pay.”

The Rockets, wearing robes or kimonos, their hair in huge rollers, all opened beers and looked for a place to sit. Donna, however, wore a western shirt, jeans, and cowgirl boots. Mascara was running down her cheeks.

She spoke in an unusually soft voice. “Girls, you all played well tonight. I’m so damned proud of you all. I’ve never had a better bunch of basketball players. You gave those people their money’s worth, not just tonight, but every night on this tour. But the gate just hasn’t been what it should have been. And the schools keep squeezing us to use their gyms. I just talked to Mel. The bank turned him down for a loan that would have gotten us into the last part of the season, and hopefully some better gates. We just can’t go on.”

Some of the Rockets had begun to cry; all looked stupefied. Charlene quickly flared up. “You can’t just say ‘good-bye and good luck.’ You owe us!”

Donna said, “I’ve got to go pick up Mel in Springfield. The bank repo’d his car.” She dropped the plastic pouch onto the bed. “I’m leaving tonight’s gate for you all to split. It ought to be a little over $500. I managed to get out without leaving the cut for the police charity, but the high school took their $100. There ought to be enough to get you all bus tickets wherever you need to go, and then some. God love you all. I'm gonna miss you." She started hugging her players.

Charlene shook her off. "Shit!"

"I'm sorry, Char." Donna picked up the keys to the panel truck and walked out. Charlene threw her half-empty beer can at the door as Donna closed it just in time.

"She can't just leave us here like this," Robin wailed.

"She just did," Charlene said.

Bobbie considered the matter briefly. "I guess it could be worse."

"How?" Charlene said through clenched teeth.

"What if we owned a whole bunch of stock in Aqua Net?"

Undertow

Sady Mayer Strand

You were stick bones and pointy angles,
blue-white eyes sunk in bruise.
I was broad bones, but a board,
mudwater eyes fighting all ways.
We were
strangers both
caught
by a station wall's burlesque
shadowdance
before light slid,
and by some legerdemain,
we saw the River's bend
in bore-down sun that
overexposed current and sky
to picked-clean
oneness.
But magic ain't for shadows only.
Blade and burning handshake
spelled us
blood brothers.
Only I weren't no boy.
And you were a bad one.
And we were caught
like things stolen, secret and sunk,
transforming themselves
on the River's floor.
Unmoved.

The Levees That Break

Sady Mayer Strand

The longest night—the night of the stand-still sun—the world turned upside down to set mine straight. That's how I tell it, my coming-on-Christmas miracle in snow, fire, and flood. On the longest night, my ancestors once lit the yule to burn for twelve days. It brought fortune in the coming year and protection from evil. Hard to imagine evil in that across-the-water island sounding like a poem spoke out loud. Hard to imagine it where I thought I found it, the land my family settled oak rings ago: Missouri, sounding like the wind through pines and Sioux for river of the big canoes. Evil was right real when I was a sapling, but once I was grown, evil fell apart. It was a straw man. It was crumbling driftwood at the river's edge. Evil was only mess and hurt and drawing breath. The rest was sleight of hand, but I didn't know it to be. Then, evil was a place or direction—north and south, mountain and river—to be rescued from.

In those years my heart prayed to be delivered from what I thought to be evil, darkness rooted deep into Our Damned Mountain among layers of rock and abandoned mines. Our mountain wasn't Damned for the evil I thought had burrowed there, but because no other word rightly described its majesty in the face of all its impossibilities. Roba Bone—my great-grandmother and the reason for this tale's telling—proclaimed regularly when I was crooked-toothed and apron-high: "Our Damned Mountain. Damned rough, damned cold in winter, but god-damned beautiful and one-half ours to birth, breed, and bury Bones."

On the miracle night, I was twelve years past the birth part. I hadn't bred, but I'd done the doing that does that. I had already buried some, and at the time of the hardest praying, the notion had set in: some folks needs killing, and some of those are kin.

My blood had come. I recall holding up wet fingertips to clouded moonlight through cracked panes, inspecting the thick scarlet, knowing it made me a woman according to men. This red held a power: It could have changed up my uncle's plans. Hell, it sure could have changed up mine if one of his payin' had dumped a baby in me. Pondering womanhood and a whole mess more, I first spied it: Flashlights carving a path to an outhouse? Car lights up the pass? Fox eyes reflecting light from burning trash? The light picked its way across the dark mountain, steadily approaching the house while I watched from window glass marked by ice stars. I wanted to look away from the light coming because it tugged on a place in my brain where I split mountain life from wishful thinking and fairytales, but I also wanted to watch. Accidents on the two-lane with red lights flashing on bare trees and metal and nothing clean—they spelled me the same: wanted to look away, but wanted to watch. I couldn't peel my eyes off the light, and hour by hour, it headed for the house. Uncle Best had been past drunk asleep in the front room. He snored and coughed over television fuzz. I was caught—frozen as the front yard— in the middle of a ghost light marching through snow mist and the bear in the front room. Asleep though he was, he made terror. Behind his moving eyelids, he dreamt a world of hurt for me.

The light took its time, picking a path above snow powder. At some point I knew the truth of it: the light was Roba come back from the grave that let go of her. She drifted over creek gravel and barbed wire, bathing clotheslines and smoldering trash bins in glow, but she didn't stir the dogs none. What could fry a man bug-eyed shitless, a chained dog accepted as the way of the seen world and the one unseen. Ain't no difference to the starved and kicked. Singing kept me calm at twelve years like cutting did. I might have sung while I drew circles in the frosted glass and waited for her to catch up to me. Not carols; ballads: "He told her to meet him at Adam's Spring; He promised her money and other fine things." Those songs lullabied mountain folk long before men drove coal carts or broke earth for towns. When I was a small bump under her quilt my mama sang them too, her warm breath forming cold verses about what a man could do to a woman in the world he'd built.

Before that night, flesh-and-blood Roba had only spoke once to me. No Bone spoke to her unless she asked for words. And she only asked when she married, buried, or sentenced. Under no circumstance did a Bone fix on her eyes. I never did, but I knew they were the same as mine: storm-sky blue with earth shot through. Some say a woman is what a man makes of her, except no man made Roba. Ever. She made all of us, like Adam passing out ribs, but also like hands making puppets walk on wood. We had no rulebook to follow save the one her and the mountain had bred into our blood. Before I could read, Roba caught me looking through her screen door at the colored bottles and papers tall as people in her front room. Gravel crunched under her boots behind me before she pulled me off the ground by my hair. I remember being surprised by the strength. Youth reckons age brings feebleness, but I learned by the pull—years made her strong. At ninety she was an oak. Her gloved hand held warmth from some animal's blood. She spoke low: "Don't whimper through it, girl. Bite your lip and take leave to that place in your head. There'll be worse. It's promised." After the last word, she let go and walked away, wiping blood and hair on her apron. I sat in the dirt watching her grow small at the tree line. She was a white spot before I got up and ran home.

Worse. Worse don't happen overnight. It takes its years, combining bad blood with bad timing. Bad luck plays a part, too. Worse turned out to be Roba's own son, the last born and sure to be her Best, and so she named him. Uncle Best, the worst Bone to live and breathe our side of the mountain. When Roba died, he worsened or simply showed his truth out from under her stare. Even on the hard rock mountain, there was a line. He'd jumped it. From the outside he looked hippie, but inside no kindness or Hare Krishna in him, only black lungs and a hole where a heart ought to be. At twelve, I was stuck in my own worst. I would my momma hadn't died because something quit in the back of her heart. I would my daddy hadn't died that day too while he still took breath morning and night before he stopped it on his own. I would my daddy never lost the house to Best. I would my daddy hadn't offered me up at ten to Best on account the house weren't enough. And I would I weren't young enough to be worth something that would never land in my hands, and instead my uncle's.

There were things a young heart shouldn't have known, but did: how the pills the payin' brought made my heart drum fast, the rhythmic click clack of the coal train skirting the mountain and speeding through our town that don't matter. How grabbing hands and bellies pushed into my hips and ribs because they don't matter. How the lawnmower blade lassoed over Best's head when outliers wanted to meddle in Bone business. And the trash bin out back, what he burnt there, the smell of it.

Hard to believe, but me and him had fair times. To make it through, you make it fair, not even, but fair-skies-and-sunshine fair. I remember when the Chevy's wheels hugged highway shoulder to keep us from leaving blacktop and taking flight over the ridge to the gully below. His hands left the wheel to yank my tank straps, pulling me up to a full sit from prying toenail paint and staring at the floor mat: "This, HoneyBaby, is important. Sit up and let it draw you. Shut your eyes." When I did, the truck filled with a whiskey warmth sound; it washed over. The asshole was right. The slow dragging beat and wail had baptizing magic: "If it keeps on raining, the levee's gonna break..." We were part of a moment, witnessing something fine. Don't everything break? A levee, a heart, time? Everything's either gonna break or be done broke. Somewhere in him, Best was broke from a bat. Someone close did it. I heard it spoke, but not from him.

Once, I ran and made it to the crossing station where I could sleep in the bathroom until sun. But when I heard the station bell sound from my spot under the sink, I knew the pock-faced boy would hand him the other key. He laughed to see me there, ready to sleep on pee: "HoneyBaby, I'm better than the shitter ain't I?" Then, he kicked me until my mind slept, taking leave the way Roba taught me. When I woke, I didn't do the work for a whole week. Instead, I nursed a map of bruises the color of Northern Lights I had seen in a magazine. Those bruises saddled up to the pink half-moons on my thighs where he ground cigarette butts in the game where I flinch, he'd burn deeper. Ever since, I had kept a bag under my bed.

I waited hours for her by the window: the time it took for the moon to arc over the pine ridge and land at the edge of a snow fog pinked by town lights. Roba stopped plain in the yard and announced her arrival: summer bugs whirring unnaturally in winter. Shrill and high, the warning wouldn't peak. The sound was all—the sound of all things together since time began—and it drew me out despite better judgment to stand before her barefoot in the snow. She was nothing but giant wings spun out through snow gusts; she enfolded me in them. I have never belonged anywhere else on this earth like I did the moment in her wings, pungent like feathers of fresh game trailing blood behind bootheels. They folded and released, creating a bellows and causing a disturbance in the snow as it fell around us. The snow fell up—the only way to say what it was with words—and something got answered: my prayers and questions I hadn't asked. The answers grew me ten feet inside, but I would never be able to explain them. Not even now.

Quick quiet interrupted the unnatural locust whir. The silence meant she had gone, and the snow had begun to fall down again instead of up. My mind set to organizing thought, sense, place and time for she had sent them all spinning. They kept their course until one stayed fixed long enough for me to make sense of her gift. The barrel poked, pointing the way through snow carpet. I could still make out the name crudely carved into the stock. Forged from metal, wood, and determined hands, the beauty waited for her target.

How did fire come to lick the house siding? I don't know. It seemed like her and it seemed like me that done it. Seemed like both of us together without either lifting a finger. It got done because it had to. What I do know is how Best stopped. Full stop, midtrack. The smoke had begun to erase the house. Covering my lips and nose with a rag, I crept heel toe down the disappearing hallway to the front room where he slept easy despite coughing fits. The rise and fall of worn leather on his chest signaled such stillness in his drunken sleep that I sang softly to him as one would a baby: "She climbed up behind him and away they did go. All down to the river, where deep waters flow. All down to the river, where the deep waters flow." He coughed loudly. His eyes—same as mine, same as Roba's—fixed on my gaze, never moving to the barrel. He switched up my small understanding of things when he nodded, a motion of both consent and acceptance as if this was his plan all along. His finger helped me pull when I stalled. Only the chair rocked for a moment from the force before it stopped too, like the breath and the being.

What I will say is when he shot the bad out of his heart, a change did overtake him. Not a physical change, though it was plain: the small hole in the heart had opened wide to his back, letting in light from the woodstove behind. I could sense the unseen one: He became everything he thought he wasn't until death showed him otherwise: tall pines burdened by snow, hawk diving from sky to earth, wood spit out by an eddy to dry on a bank in the sun. I kissed him on the cheek for it.

After, me and my bag left in the truck, through the woods, turning south toward the highway along the river.

Though I was gone to have witnessed it, I knew the house burned long that night. I knew, too, it didn't matter to the mountain or its inhabitants. The snow fell heavy. The night animals burrowed and scavenged. The dogs took comfort in the heat and napped. And the Bones on the mountain side? They did not stir from Our Damned Mountain until they were sure the house was licked clean and beginning to be matted over by white—white ash combined with white snow.

Weeks later the snow brought a spring flood in the dead of winter. It broke wide. It broke wide at the heart of it.

Castle Ruins—Ha Ha Tonka State Park

Ida Fogle

The size is there still, the outline,
the height. Stone walls loom colossal,
a grand anomaly in the Ozark hills.
Grass grows where the ballroom was.
Still people come to marvel
seventy years after it burned.
The man who began this old world splendor
perished before it was done, his death
a harbinger of the future, the first
fatal car wreck in the state.
Still, his sons finished the project,
fulfilled his dream and lived there
a short while, before one died young
and then the fire sparked up.
The grounds are lovely for picnicking.
You can look through the window openings
from a safe distance behind a fence.
The drop to the former basement
is precipitous. Carriage houses are gone
with no trace, but enough of the castle
remains to be a monument of sorts
to something. Dreaming perhaps.
Or irony. Viewer's choice.

Old Lead Mine—Bonne Terre, Missouri

Ida Fogle

A hundred feet or more down on wooden ladders
And rickety stairs, then back up
After a twelve-hour day
Fill three cars and earn a dollar

Now there's a lake underground, with paid tours
On pontoon boats, life jackets provided
The water's so clear
You can see abandoned drills thirty feet below

Jacques Cousteau filmed here once
And then the scuba divers came
They still do, it's that deep
A single goldfish resides, growing and growing.

Onondaga Cave

Ida Fogle

This race is indeed not to the swift
and is not a race.
Today we like speed. The whole world
in an instant with a keystroke.
Third-graders: do 100 addition problems
in five minutes. Speed proves competence.
Service so quick you'll quake,
or something like that.
Nobody should wait.
The gravest sin is to slow others down.
That's above ground.

Enter this cave and the standards invert.
Muse upon the mighty stalagmites.
Take in the tightly clinging stalactites.
Marvel at the pace of growth, an inch per year.
One. Inch. Per. One. Year.
That's where the awe comes in.
If they formed at a fast clip, we'd chop them out,
carry them off, stack them in our garages,
intending to use them in a craft some day.
There would be no sense of wonder.
The slowness makes it so.
Speed wins the day, persistence the millennia.

When Pigs Fly

Carol Gorski Buckels

Once upon a time, there was a little Red Wattle pig boar named Bob. He lived on a farm in Buffalo, Missouri, and roamed the fields, rooting and foraging with the other pigs, but Bob had his dreams—dreams of flying. The other pigs watched Bob as he lay on a knoll watching eagles circling overhead. The other pigs thought that Bob was a fool. They kept to the shallows and wallows among the trees.

Eagle Bluff Farm was known for its view of the bluffs above the Niangua River. Grass and bamboo grew thick. The pigs had pasture land, a lake, and a nice stash of hot dog casings interred about the property. In a spasm of corporate logic, the local hot dog company had skirted the laws and, instead of properly disposing of the casings, had buried them. The company reimbursed the property owners, an unsuspecting older woman and her sister, for use of their land as a dump site. Eventually the biodegradable casings would dissolve, but for now they were the cause of a pitched battle between the Department of Natural Resources and the hot dog factory.

Bob, as a pig, had a destiny, and that destiny was not flight, but to become fodder for the factory. Of course, the pigs did not know this and ate and grew fat, except for Bob, who watched and pined and ran very fast about the pasture, sometimes taking flying leaps off the knoll after he had watched a particularly thrilling eagle flight.

The eagles caught the air currents with their wings. They swooped and soared in circles. People came to watch with binoculars and were inspired.

One day, Bob caught the eye of a passing eagle as he leaped from his knoll. Leaping as he did, Bob did not look much like a rabbit, but this was a rather lazy and near-sighted eagle. He swooped in and grabbed Bob and off they went into the sky, Bob squealing with shock and yet delight at being airborne, not yet quite sure what was happening to him.

The other pigs were shocked as well. No eagle had ever grabbed a pig from their field before. They shook their heads. They knew how this would end.

"Here pig, pig, pig," called their owner that night. "Let's fatten you up a bit more. Tomorrow is market day." She spread the grain and the pigs crowded around, still murmuring about poor Bob and his untimely end. They ate with gusto, unaware of their own ride that had been arranged for the following morning. They ate with the assurance of those who know how the world works, safe in the knowledge that smart pigs don't fly, they chew.

The next morning, the truck pulled up. Some men herded the pigs aboard for their ride to the slaughterhouse.

"When do you think we will make enough to buy this place?" the son asked the father. The truck windows were rolled down, and the breeze carried his answer back to the pigs, who pondered its meaning.

"When pigs fly," the father growled.

Up the road, another farmer contemplated giving up the life after what he had seen the day before. After too long a day on the tractor he had looked into the sky, just into the sun, as Bob soared past. The farmer didn't dare tell anyone, not even his wife. But he did mention the possibility of retirement, much to his wife's surprise.

Defiance

Carol Gorski Buckels

I drove into the storm with rain
and clouds so dark and
wicked it seemed as if
the darkness of all past nights
had united to shut out
any glimpse of haven.

Only flashes of lightning
kept me from running off the edge
of that familiar road. I couldn't stop
not knowing who or what was behind me
yet there was no road ahead.

With shoulders tight and hunched,
and eyes strained from searching
the darkness, I inched forward.
The half-bent windshield wipers
slapped crazily, uselessly,
lost on the road home.

Float Trip

Carol Gorski Buckels

We are floating the Jacks Fork
River, down the valley
through rapids, past
half-sunken logs.

Red sand cliffs
shade this seething river,
running aqua
green
and clear.

I see each dark
rock on the river floor
but I can't see
round the bend.

Is the left channel filled
with snags?
Is there an opening?
Can we float through the
rapids in the right-hand
channel? Will
the rushing current
grab us, push us into
a grasping bush,
flip us into roaring, cold water?

Is that a rock
where the water is swirling?
No! A dark, old tree
that tries to catch us as we
slip past on the side!

We choose, paddle and forge ahead,
choose and forge ahead.

Paddle hard on the left!
Rock ahead!

Snag!
Shallows! Paddle right!
Wait!
But we can't wait.

The current pushes us
forward. There is no
stopping mid-river.

Catching our breath
on a gravel bar
we turn and see
a white stallion
picking his way to
the water's edge from the woods.
His long, sleek mane
gives him the look
of a dream.

He steps into the shallows
followed closely by two
white mares, then a pinto,
a black horse, more white mares
a brown mare, a foal.
A wild herd of 13.

We are in the exact right spot
at the exact right time.
This is Missouri's last
wild horse herd and we
are here to see it.

What current pulled us
to this place to see
wild horses drinking
in a wild river
on a summer's day?

The Ride

Emme Hanson

"It's fucking hot," I say as soon as Mary picks up.

"No, shit, Jess."

I am sitting in the piano chair in the living room. The phone cord barely stretches from the kitchen. The piano didn't come with a bench when the church gave it to us.

"What are you doing?" I ask.

"Nothing. This summer is more boring than school."

The top of the piano collects things, a box of Christmas stuff that should be in the attic, placemats for the kitchen table, the handwritten pages to bring to Jude.

"We could try to find someone to buy us some beer," she says. "What are you doing?"

"I don't know. Jude's supposed to be picking me up."

"When?"

"Like two hours ago."

"To do what?"

"I don't know. I wish I had a license." I hit a couple of gloomy notes on the piano.

"Yeah, me too. I want a license that says I'm 21."

"Please, you don't look 16."

"Shit, I'm almost 17," she said.

"But still no license." I walk back to the kitchen.

"What would we do if I had a license?" she asks.

"I don't know, go somewhere. Anywhere that's not 15 miles from town."

"With what car?"

"Shit. Any car. You think your parents are going to help you get one?"

"Who knows? They're all about *get a job, get your own car.* You think I can get a job without a car? Where? All that's around here is a bunch of fields and too many trees."

I stretch the phone cord into the bathroom. I look in the mirror and pull my hair away from my sweaty neck. I often stand in front of the mirror while I talk on the phone. It's not that I'm impressed by my reflection—same dark hair and pale skin, same green eyes. Some boys say I'm pretty, but it could be a line, who knows? I like to watch my expressions change as I talk, to practice for times I talk to people, to know what I look like when I tell a story or make a joke.

Mary sighs. "Would your mom take us somewhere?"

"She's not here. Gone all weekend." I scowl, narrow my eyes. I like the dramatic expressions. They're the best for my rather plain face. "Dad's at the farm stand."

"You wanna meet halfway?" she asks.

Sometimes we walk toward each other, meeting up after a couple of miles in the middle. But then we're on a dirt road through the woods with nothing to do. And I'm too agitated for a walk. "I wish he'd get here."

"You gonna have sex with him soon?"

"I don't know. It's complicated," I say. "You know." I close my eyes and walk away from the mirror.

"Well, do you want to? He's cute."

"But I don't think he believes me about what happened with Devon."

"Maybe you should just break up with him."

"I don't want to break up with him. I shouldn't have to break up with him because of Devon. Hasn't he fucked up my life enough?"

"They've been friends for a long time."

"Nobody should be friends with that asshole." I shove the front door open and pace across the porch. "He doesn't deserve a single friend. He doesn't deserve to be friends with a fucking bait worm." The phone cord stretches behind me like an angry tail, twitching the screen door back and forth.

"I don't think you even like Jude."

"Why?"

"You said so, when we were at the lake."

"I did?" I ask. "I was drunk. I didn't mean it." A car goes by. It isn't Jude. But he might be here soon. I'm nervous. "I'm going to show him that story I wrote about Devon and all that shit."

"You think he'll believe it?"

"He'll have to believe it. I couldn't have written it like that if it didn't really happen."

"What if he shows Devon?" she asks.

"I'll fucking kill him."

"Who?"

"Both of them."

She sighs. "We could walk to the river."

"Too many drunk rednecks there. You think I shouldn't show him?"

"I don't know, Jess..."

"I'm going to show him."

"What if he doesn't read it?"

"He's gotta believe me."

"Shit, someone's beeping in," she says. "Hold on." The phone clicks.

I pull weeds from between the steps and twist them into a small wreath. No cars go by.

When she comes back, she says, "Hey, it's Mom's work. I'll call you back."

"I'll be here, unless Jude shows up."

Twenty minutes go by. Three cars go by. I have been waiting too long. I go back to the phone and dial Jude's number. It's usually him who calls me. There's never much to say. Sometimes I walk to his house just to have somewhere to go. It takes a couple of hours and sometimes he's not home.

His father answers, his gruff voice nearly yelling into the phone.

"Hey, is Jude there?" I am feeling very light, woozy.

"Jessie?"

"Yeah."

"Well, ya missed him, girl. He went to the river a couple hours ago."

"Oh, he was going to come pick me up."

"Aggh, that car's shit. Devon came over to work on it but they gave up."

"He went to the river with Devon?" I do not feel light anymore. There is blood pounding in my ears. Someone laughs in the background.

I pick up a small kitchen knife, make a fist around it, put it back down.

"Jessie? You there?"

I hang up.

I try to stop, to think or breathe. I find that I cannot. My father's hunting things are in the basement. I know how to shoot a gun. But I can't walk to the river with a rifle over my shoulder. Unless I cut through the woods. But I don't open the gun cabinet.

Instead I take the gutting knife and leather holder. It is not much bigger than the kitchen knife, but sharper.

I fasten the sheath to my cut-offs so that it rests against my leg with only the belt clip showing. When I slip the knife in the end rests just under my lower ribs. It looks awkward, somewhat obvious against my boney pelvis. I put on a bikini top and baggy t-shirt, pull my hair back.

I just need them to know.

The screen door slams behind me. The hot air seems to spark my anger, push me through the neighborhood, along the roughly paved road, past places of childhood, past ugly, leering memories.

How could he? How could either of them not see? Believe that anything would be ok?

I could cut through the corn to my right, get there a little faster, but the corn is high. I keep to the road, looking to the next bend. I hear a car, not Jude, but it could be someone I know, the parent of a friend or the friend of a relative.

Not wanting to be seen, I step into the corn, go back a few rows and try to crouch. The knife pulls against my shorts and I end up planting my knee in the dry, cracked soil.

When the car passes, I push through the corn again. I walk awkwardly, hiding the knife, favoring my knee. Everything is heat, pain and anger.

I wish I could shed the t-shirt, which clings to the sweat along my lower back, pulls at my skin, but I must hide the knife. Sweat leaks into thin slashes from the leaves of the corn.

A very small wind meanders through the field, shuffling the leaves and tassels of the corn. I don't feel it, not even one little puff.

The anger doesn't fade. All I think about is the betrayal. It was bad enough that Jude didn't believe me, even worse that he wanted to remain friends with Devon. This though, leaving me waiting, choosing Devon over me, this is too much.

Devon doesn't deserve to be alive, unless rotting in some ill-maintained prison, or being horribly disfigured and crippled in some freak accident. Instead he is free, thriving, spending time with my boyfriend....

It just can't go on. There is a point when failure to stand up for yourself becomes an admission of weakness. No way am I going to go let people keep hurting me, taking me for granted. If

Jude never talks to me again, oh well. If they lock me up in some loony bin or send me to the school for troubled kids, fine. At least I'll be safe when people know not to mess with me. When they fear me.

These thoughts carry me to the small dirt road to the river, dust and gravel pressed into two thin hard paths by countless summers of pickup trucks, old work vans, rusted cars. The river is for locals only, for men who pass out beers to anyone who can open them, for teenagers hiding in the woods smoking joints, for young mothers skinny dipping and for grandmothers herding children away from the wide banks and the mischief.

It will be busy on such a hot day. My revenge depends on getting Devon away from the crowd...

A pickup sways toward me, the back heavy with sunburned bodies. They are laughing, teasing an older girl walking on the path. The truck matches her pace. A guy helps her up into the bed, dropping his beer in the process.

The truck rollicks across the creaking bridge. The sunburned driver guides the tires along the boards while holding his beer out the window and belching. I wait quietly in the tall grass, resist swatting at a bug humming around my ear. The truck dips into the ruts where the boards end. Beer spills from the can and a man in the back yells, "Beer shocks!" People laugh. No one notices me.

I'm carried forward by my anger. How many people will be there? Who else will I know? I think that it will work out, somehow. It is meant to be. I will find my opportunity, my revenge.

A dense row of pine and underbrush between me and the river keep me from seeing it until I reach the opening to the gravel parking lot. The trees give an out-of-place holiday smell to the thick air.

The river is empty. I jog forward. No one is in sight. How could it be? They couldn't have left before I got here. Dust settles silently around me. Rusty metal barrels on the edge of the parking lot overflow with bottles and cans. It's impossible, there should be dozens of people here.

Yet, no one is.

I walk up and down the bank, listening for any sound of life, hearing only the current. I am the only one here, and the cool rush of the river invites me. The grass banks slope to large river-worn rocks. I sit to remove my high tops and slip my feet into the edge of a deep pool where the water gathers and waits before running through the next curve. I look around again. I take off the knife and holster, then wrap it in my shirt, and leave it carefully balanced on a rock nearby.

I dive in and emerge; the sweat washed away, my skin cool. I swim back and forth, then float, staring at the blue sky, like a misted lake above me. A speck of silver plane moves silently along the sky. Each time the current sucks my ankles forward, I do a couple of backstrokes toward the center of the pool. Tiny drops fall from my arms, temporary glistening jewels.

Eventually, I swim back and pull myself out of the water onto the sun-warmed rock.

I can't have this place to myself much longer. How absurd really, to have had it this long. I put the knife back, cover it with my shirt again.

The hottest part of the day has passed. It will still be light when I get home, but a little cool of evening has already settled into the shade of the dirt road as I head for home.

My wet jean shorts seem to take off tiny layers of thigh skin as I walk. They cling to the knife, push it firmly into my leg.

I feel tired now. I could walk to Mary's and try to get a ride home. Jude's house is less than a mile away, in the other direction, but clearly I can't go there. I think, maybe, I'll never go there again.

A car zips past, small and black, going a little too fast for the curving road. I don't recognize it, but I know the driver. He swerves slightly. He has seen me. But he is going fast, maybe he didn't realize it was me. Maybe I am still safe.

His brake lights flare before the next curve, the one which will carry him out of sight.

I am sweating again. Scared.

He has left Jude's, I realize. He has seen me. Or he has seen a glimpse of a girl. A baggy shirt, a sloppy wet ponytail. That's all. He was hurrying somewhere, or driving fast because he liked to. He wasn't paying attention.

But I can't forget the brake lights. I stand in the road. The trees and fields wait with me, still and silent.

"Keep driving," I whisper. I can't hear the engine. Blood is pounding in my ears.

I could hide, but here isn't time. He has turned around.

My hand goes to the knife, the handle under my shirt, near the sudden pain in my stomach.

I stop touching the knife, act natural as possible.

He is still going fast, right past me, recognition clear in his snide smile.

I think I might throw up, seeing that satisfied look on his face. I know now that he will be back. He could run me right over, I think. He would if he knew what I had come here to do.

I walk.

The car again, I don't even look, hearing the engine behind me. He is going slowly this time. Excruciating.

I walk. With each step, I feel the knife against tender skin and the scrape of still wet denim between my legs. I sense the warmth of the sun from his hood as he lingers right behind me. I take a few last steps.

He inches forward. He is beside me. He leans across the passenger seat, rolls the window further down to yell over the noise of the old engine.

"Do you need a ride?"

Saying Goodbye to an Ozark Original

Tracy Barnett

Oh come, Angel Band
Come and around me stand
Oh bear me away on your snowy wings
To my immortal home,
Oh bear me away on your snowy wings
To my immortal home.

Roselle, Iron County, Missouri—Redbud blossoms splashed the spring-green hills the day my mother called me home from Guatemala. The freshness in the air and the gentleness of the colors were medicine to my eyes, and yet they pained me, knowing as I did how my grandfather loved this time of year.

Normally, I thought, he would be out on his Missouri Century Farm planting right now, or standing on the banks of an Ozark stream or pond, reeling in a bucket full of fish to share with family and friends.

He was struggling to manage basic functions when I finally reached his bedside—breathing and swallowing were a painful chore. His already birdlike frame seemed even tinier and frailer than when I had left him in December. He was asking to be released, to be allowed to go home to his Lord.

He groaned when he saw me. "Oh, I didn't want to be such a bother," he managed to get out.

"Grandpa, it's not a bother, it's a gift," I protested. "You know how much I love to come see you in the springtime. The redbud is blooming and it's so beautiful!"

"Those sure were some good nuts you brought up," he said, remembering the bag of Texas pecans I'd picked up on my last trip from Houston.

Grandpa spent his winters picking out walnuts and hickory nuts that he'd gathered on his farm, and he filled bags with them to distribute among family and friends. This had been a dry year and the harvest was thin, so Texas pecans filled in for Ozark hickories. It wasn't much, but I was glad for it.

His last days were that way—filled with remembrances for each of his grandchildren, great-grandchildren and great-great-grandchildren, with words of appreciation for the tiny things we did. My mother and her sisters and brother hovered nearby, knowing that each word he spoke cost him dearly.

My grandfather the storyteller asked me to tell him about my trip. I did my best, describing the mountains, the jungle, the birds of Guatemala. Maybe I was too enthusiastic in my descriptions, because my aunt came in and put her hand on my shoulder.

"He needs to rest," she whispered. Grandpa didn't miss a beat.

"I'm talking to Tracy," he rasped.

"Oh! OK," said my aunt and retreated respectfully.

My sister came in with an arrangement of redbuds beautiful as a poem.

"I just want to go sing praises to the Lord forever and ever," he told my father.

I swabbed his parched mouth with water as the family gathered.

One by one my sisters and my aunt began to sing "Angel

Band," and I felt the angels gathering in the background. The next day, he was gone.

~

Chris Lloyd "Pete" Hicks was born to a dirt-poor farmer and trapper in the Missouri Ozarks on Nov. 7, 1917. Grandpa's mother, our great-grandmother Esta Stahl, daughter of a German immigrant, had come to these parts from the Ohio foothills in a covered wagon when she was only two. Her father fought in the Civil War right here in these Ozark hills. Grandpa's father, Jesse Hicks, had accompanied his own father, William, to Cripple Creek, Colorado during the gold rush days and they had earned enough to buy the farm. But farming wasn't for Jesse, and when he grew up he let the farm run down while he trapped furs for a living.

As a young boy in the Great Depression, Grandpa was pressed into service with his father, and he told us stories of rising at dawn to hunt with his father, then going to school with the stink of animals on his clothing. He learned to laugh about it. His stories always drew a crowd—stories about carving out a life in the wilderness, about rising above hardship, about outsmarting rivals, about working hard but always taking time to have a laugh.

I asked him once if he'd known any moonshiners there in the Ozark Hills, which were famous for their illicit whiskey production during the Prohibition.

"Well, some people called 'em criminals, but sometimes they was just good people tryin' to provide for their families," he told me.

Turns out some of those good people were his uncles, and he told of the elaborate system they'd devised to conceal their labors. When the "Revenuers" came over the hill on a raid, someone was always on the lookout, and the trap door would come down over the still. Nobody was ever caught.

Grandpa told with a mischievous grin about when he and his friends would sneak into the barn to make off with a little of that "mountain dew." But one of his friends died after drinking too much of a bad batch, and he steered clear of the stuff after that. Or so he told me.

Grandpa was as devout and humble a churchgoing man as you'd ever meet. He was a deacon at New Hope Primitive Baptist Church and he never missed a meeting; he loved the singing and the preaching and the fellowship as much as he loved anything.

"Keep looking up," was his most frequent advice to me. He wasn't one to wear his religion on his sleeve, as Brother Travis Eye said at his memorial service. Instead, he lived his faith every day, dedicating his life to the service of others—friends and family alike. He lived in gratitude, celebrating the joy of a sunrise, a good catch, an abundant harvest, a visiting grandchild.

At Grandpa's funeral, we met a friend of his that he loved like a son—Chris Schillinger, the owner of Baylee Jo's Bar-B-Q and Grill in Ironton. My sisters and I had heard about Chris over the years, a fishing buddy who took him camping and whitewater rafting when Grandpa was in his 80s. But it wasn't until Chris invited us all to his restaurant for a sumptuous home-style dinner after Grandpa's funeral service—about 150 of us, and then he refused to take a dime—that we met this remarkable man, and we got a glimpse into a different side of Grandpa.

"Your grandpa was a heck of a man," Chris declared, with tears in his eyes. "You know, he never judged me. I was a single dad, and I had a few girlfriends, but he never cared about that."

He showed us the place near the cash register, behind the bar, where he would hang our grandfather's photo, right next to that of another buddy who had died.

There were a few stories he could tell us sometime, he went on, but maybe not now. The crowd fresh from the church milled around outside while the tattooed bikers dined inside. We begged him to tell.

"I don't know how you'll feel about this, but your grandpa liked to have a beer or two every now and again," he began. Not a secret, but not exactly his public image. "Well, once he told me about the bottle of whiskey he used to keep up in the barn—he said, 'I'd drink just a little bit in the winter to warm me up. But when July rolled around and I was still drinking it, I knew I had to quit!'"

As Chris spoke, the Norman Rockwell watercolor of our grandfather faded and a real flesh-and-blood human being with all his strengths and foibles came into rare view. We laughed together and loved him all the more.

We went to Grandpa's house after the dinner, a beautiful home he had built for my grandmother from pink Ozark granite. Tuckpointed in white and framed with two tall oaks, the home has been a picturesque part of the scenery in these parts for three generations. The tulips he planted in front of the house swayed in the breeze, and the birds he loved sat in the branches above, waiting, perhaps, for him to come fill their feeders.

All his children and most of his 48 grandchildren, great-grandchildren and great-great-grandchildren were there. We walked across the fields he had nurtured with his own sweat, and we took turns choosing mementos from his belongings.

It was a heartfelt evening and we wavered, as we had all week, between sorrow and joy. Grandpa was where he wanted to be, and he was still giving to us. Cousins, nieces and nephews, aunts and uncles reconnected after years apart. Children and grandchildren looked through his pocketknife collection, his tools, his books, Grandma's dishes and knickknacks, each of them just as likely to find something for someone else as for themselves. Giving was the order of the day.

I chose a couple of photos of Grandpa, a couple of pocket knives, a Zane Grey novel and a John Deere pillow my aunt Cheri had made for him. I slept with that pillow, and the next morning, I awoke with the sunrise, as Grandpa always did. I felt his presence powerfully, and he was everywhere.

Our little grandpa isn't little anymore, I realized, and I smiled.

Earl's Barn

Jim Coffman

Didya hear 'bout Earl's barn?
Burned last night
clean to the cement floor.
Just finished farrowin'
the last two hogs,
two good litters, he said.
Heat lamp too close
to the straw, I guess.
Pity to see Earl
shufflin' 'round
with his corn scoop
movin' them gray ashes
and lumps of lard around,
grown man blubberin'
'bout his winter's work.
Shame to see
that pile o' ashes
where his barn was
last night

Mr. & Mrs. Wilson

Steve Gallagher

I wasn't even in school yet, and I could stand in the back of the Mercury with my hands on Mom's seat. We turned off the country road and headed down the driveway to Mr. and Mrs. Wilson's house. It was a very long driveway, possibly once a county road itself. We passed through a dense, brushy stand of blackjack oaks, went down a hill and then rounded the corner past Ibbie Johnson's tall brown house where Ibbie's daughter, who was in her early 80s, also lived. Then our car went between a creek on one side and a meadow on the other. Big potholes full of water pitted the road. Even though we crept along, the deep holes sent me up off my feet and I was thrilled, eagerly anticipating each new pond. Water splashed the muffler, leaving a vaporous trail. I thought we were a steam engine.

At the end of the road, we stopped near a small white house with a tin roof. It was perched at the bottom edge of a steep slope where the hill met the creek. Goats grazed on the hillside. Inside the house was Mrs. Wilson. I was always sure she was an angel, though a very skinny one, with a thin face and boney hands, and wearing a very pretty apron. She had the habit of giving me sweet things from her kitchen and of giving coffee to the adults, her shaky hands spilling a little of the curious adult drink onto the saucer as she carried it to each person.

We went to what used to be the living room, but had turned to a bedroom. "Bill," she said, "this is Stevie. Betty's son." She said this in a loud voice and took me over and had me shake his hand. I don't recall what that felt like to my hand. I was occupied with his milky, bluish eyes, staring into the emptiness. I think he could see light, maybe a bit more. The dim room smelled like an old house. Mr. Wilson sat in a big chair, as if he'd always been there, looking kind of grouchy. If he said anything to me, I don't recall it.

Later, Mom told me something which had happened to Mr. Wilson many years before. A big storm was coming, and he had been hurrying to put the horses and harnesses away. A huge bolt of lightning came down and hit the barn. The blast was so great that Mr. Wilson's eyeballs were knocked onto his cheeks! He escaped the barn, but it burned down, killing everything in it. His eyes had to be put back in their sockets by a doctor, and after that, he had only a fraction of the sight he'd had before.

Except for Mr. Wilson, the rest of the household went to the Church of the Nazarene. Me and my parents went, too, when we were visiting, which was often. In that church, everyone prayed out loud, all at once. Some were quieter, some very loud and emotional. Uncle Job was one of the loud ones. He was creative in his gratitude to the Lord. And after anyone's prayer, the parishioners would say, "And *Lord*! We'll be careful to give you the *Glory*!" These folks had ways to stretch words which no one else on Earth can do. And they were diligent to avoid the eternal fires of Hell and to rest finally in the arms of Jesus on that great Judgment Day.

My grandma told me what happened when Mr. Wilson eventually died. As he lay on his deathbed, he kept saying, "The fires! Oh, the fires!" The relatives, the Christians, all looked at each other knowingly. After that, they were even more vigilant to please the Lord, with whom they intended to live for eternity.

December

Kathleen Cain

You cross the creek
Notice that the park is empty
Last night's rains have left pooling water
On saturated ground

The path through the woods is moving
A stream, making its way, snakelike, down to the swollen creek
Flowing below the bluffs

Deep into the woods traffic sounds grow dim
Replaced by the sound of the flood
Churning brown and menacing below

On your right
As you traverse the ridge
He appears
How long has he been with you?
You can't say

"Are you limping?" he whispers
"A bit," I reply. "Probably the damp."
"Arthritis," he comments.
"Natural, as you age."

Is that a smile, or a leer?

“Not now,” he whispers.
“But I won’t wait forever, you know.”
A bony finger scolds, as he backs into the undergrowth
Disappears.

White sycamores rise
Above dark timber
Winter’s bones.

More rain is forecast.

DEEP WINTER

Kathleen Cain

It may not be cold this year
But the days are still short
Night descends from heavy cloud covers
Leaving us to plan and cook in the dark

A time of reflection
Perhaps dread
As winters stack one upon another

Accordions, unplayed
They acquire dust and portent

Of this life
A solemn thing
So private

We say goodbye to those who leave it
Contemplate our own passing
But only on the surface
As spiders skimming a pond in early spring

I walk in the hardwoods
Barks soaked in cold rain

A wind passed through last night
And I step around small branches
Throw some aside

Delight in my dog's pursuit of squirrels
Until I think of her success
A small body, limp in her jaws

As though I don't shop for meat

This brutal, precious, delicious life

My aloneness startles me at times

A Jacks Fork Easter

Julie Gardner

"When you do things from your soul,

you feel a river moving in you, a joy."

-Rumi

A river is a wild thing, especially when it rises. Like the Niangua, Current and Jacks Fork rivers where I canoed the Missouri Ozarks, in my teen years I was not always containable. Somewhere between childhood and adulthood, I was trying to decide who I was without the limits given to me by authority figures: Mom, Dad, Roman Catholic religion, teachers, and the boss at the restaurant where I waitressed.

My earliest memories are saying grace around our large maple-Formica table: nine children and two parents with prayer-folded hands, reciting *Bless us O Lord, ... through Christ, our Lord, Amen.* I attended Catholic schools from first through twelfth grade; went to daily Mass; lit Advent wreath candles; put hay in the manger for baby Jesus when I did a good deed. I filled my milk carton-like box with coins for the hungry during Lent, and was terrified of my first confession, afraid I'd go blank and forget all my sins. My older brother eased my angst when he said, "At the end just say for these and all the sins I've forgotten."

I felt like a holy princess on the day of my first communion, and I researched saints for my confirmation name, choosing

St. Thérèse of Lisieux. Like her, I wanted to be a cloistered nun married only to God—one who wrote poems and love letters to God. That didn't last long—at least the "married only to God" part. In tenth grade, a force stronger than my saintly resolve came over me. I had a keen interest in boys—one in particular.

My initiation to canoeing came when I joined my Catholic high school's club. It wasn't the river I was attracted to. At that time, I didn't know the river. I had recently moved from California to Kansas, so I was more at home with the sea. Joining the canoe club was a way I could be with John, my boyfriend, as we canoed the Niangua and Current Rivers.

At age seventeen, my boyfriend and I were engaged, planning to get married in August just before we headed to Kansas State. To this date, forty years later, I wonder how we convinced our parents to let us go on a float trip. Not only were we going as minors with another underage couple, we were going on Easter weekend. I think we told our parents we'd go to Easter Mass at the Chapel on the Lake.

We went to the Jacks Fork, putting in at the Highway 17 Bridge and floated to Alley Spring. Along the way we would camp, then get shuttled back to our car on Easter. There had been recent rains. The gradient was steep, the water high. It made it easier to get through the usual shallow rocky areas where we'd sometimes have to get out of our canoe and portage. I took the front. My role was to scout conditions and let John know when there was a tree limb, shallows or rocks coming up. As we approached one bend, I heard people hollering, then saw them gathering their belongings after they had tipped.

I warned John, "We better take the canoe out and put in beyond this tree."

He slowed the canoe, then stopped and scrutinized things for himself. On the left side of the river stood a big tree. John said, "We can do it. Just keep your paddle straight and give it plenty of power."

And so I prayed and paddled—hard.

The current was strong enough to slam us, like all others who had come before, into the downed tree, which was curved—the perfect shape to cradle and tip us all the way over. The canoe, made heavy by our Coleman cooler, took on water. After a struggle, we righted ourselves, then the canoe. While I held it steady, John swam to our gear, recovering the cooler lid and two knotted black garbage bags that did absolutely nothing to keep our tent, sleeping bags and clothes dry.

Late in the afternoon, we found a gravel bar to set up camp, and pitched our tents. Near the campfire, we made a makeshift clothesline from tree branches in a failed attempt to dry our sleeping bags and clothes before we went to bed. We threw our foil packs of seasoned ground beef patties, onions, potatoes and carrots into the fire, opened a can of 3.2 Coors, and lit our Old Golds with the hot embers on the end of a stick. We ate and sang.

The fire took away my shivers. Feeling tired and relaxed, I lay back on the blanket. The stars wouldn't let me close my eyes. I prayed and started my slide into guilty thinking: thank you God for the lights in the expanse of the heavens. It's Holy Week. On Thursday, I had my feet washed in a ritual at church. On Friday, during the Stations of the Cross, I tried to imagine Jesus' pain. Now it is Holy Saturday, the time when Jesus was supposed to be in the tomb—and I am on the banks of the Jacks Fork. Tomorrow is Easter Sunday, the holiest day in the Roman Catholic Church—and I won't be at Mass.

When it was time to retire to our tent, our sleeping bags were still damp. My spirits, too. We lined our sleeping bags with black plastic trash bags. After tossing and turning for hours, tormented by relentless thoughts vacillating between Deliverance movie scenes and my imaginary Catholic devil, I was dripping wet. John said, "Condensation."

We abandoned our tent and the idea of getting any sleep, and went outside to start a new fire. Too tired for conversation, we sat side-to-side, resting our heads together. During the darkest hour before dawn I heard the howling of animals from a nearby hill.

"Wolves?" I asked. "How close?"

John assured me, "There hasn't been wolves in the Ozarks for decades. Harmless coyotes, coming from far away—across the river."

It was the hour of the wolf. I so wanted to believe him, but he had been sure we would make it through the rough waters. In that moment, I wanted to believe everything my mom, dad, religion, teachers, bosses and boyfriend said. Instead, I listened to the howling of the coyotes. In that moment, with the moon backlighting the silhouetted cottonwood trees, I became one with the coyotes (or improbable though not impossible wolves). Like them, I was howling, yearning, searching, living and loving into the mystery of the river and God. The fire was our Easter Vigil altar, the wild animals our choir. Our earlier immersion into the Jacks Fork made it possible for us to witness the dawn of that Easter morning. Though I had not slept, I awakened to a new kind of spirituality, to the wildness of Love and Mystery, to a God that is uncontainable by any church or religion. It has taken decades for me to be grateful for all that has moved me closer to me, into Mystery, to celebrate mystical experiences in nature—that joyous Easter morning on the Jacks Fork River.

The Old Road

John M. Brown

No one owns the old road,
It's been there for as long as anyone can remember.
Brown ruts slithering off
Beneath tall sugar maples.

Ribbons of field stone,
long ago stacked into walls.
Covered with weather-cracked lichens
braced snow drifts in winter
and warmed snake bellies in spring.

Horses, pulling sleighs burdened with vats of maple sap
pulling... pulling through slush melting snow,
heaved their breath into winter mornings,
down that road that no one owns.

Barefoot boys
with cane poles over shoulders,
sauntered, as mud erupted between their toes.
Boys, headed towards Maggies Swamp
where catfish pumped their gills;
waiting.

Waiting for the boys,
and their worms,
and their laughter
as lines grew taut with struggle,
and wood bent deep towards water.

Girls, fluttering in the wind
after their first kiss,
lean back against rough maple bark.
Anticipating their first foreign caress.
The closeness of breath,
fomenting in moon shadows.

Where yellow dandelions
embraced the earth
between wheels of wagons,
then automobiles

and now... nothing.

Since the creek, above bank
tore deep into the old road.

No one cares about the old road;
nor maples
or fishes
or first kisses.

Snake Handling

Nathan Boone

William Robert Ashley rocked gently in the swing that hung from the wood and tin porch overhang by two lengths of frayed jute rope. He sipped black coffee from a ceramic cup as the blue-gray light of dawn bloomed through the oaks and sycamores and shagbark hickories that towered over his little slice of Winslow Mountain.

The air smelled of wood smoke and mist, wet leaves and evergreen and bacon wafting from the kitchen. Out in the yard, clumps of fescue sprang up through the mat of leaves and fog, their tall stalks drooping under the weight of sparkling morning dew. As the first rays turned pink on the horizon, a cardinal lit with a flutter of crimson in the burning bush near the unpainted porch railing. The bush was in the middle of its fall transformation. Some leaves were summer green or bruised purple, some as red as the little bird hopping lithely from twig to twig.

The cardinal flew away and William Robert smiled and closed his eyes and began to pray.

Father, I know I'm a sinner and unworthy of this day, but by your grace I'll walk right, in praise and thanks for all the blessings you've bestowed, and I'll do your work as it's written. Please bless mama, look over her and keep her in health. Bless the congregation Lord, especially them that's fixin' to backslide. I'm awful worried about Larry Dixon and Jessica Rodes, Lord. Come into them young peoples' hearts. Lead 'em away from the devil's temptation and into the light of the church so that I may show them the power of your holiness. Also, Lord, I don't mean to be greedy, but I'm runnin' a might low on serpents, so I'm a prayin' for good weather, with lots of sunshine and rattlers today. In Jesus Christ's name, amen.

Delma poked her head outside. "Breakfast's ready."

William Robert turned his bald head over his shoulder. His face was at once infantile and middle-aged. His cheeks were fat, the skin poached pink and tight; his chin small and creased like an apricot. He offered a groggy smile, lines showing in the corners of his small brown eyes."Ok mama," he said.

Wrapping his thick fingers around the tattered King James setting next to him, William Robert stood up, the knotty, weathered planks groaning under his bulk. He followed Delma through the front room into the little threadbare kitchen and sat down at the unfinished pine dining table with the glowing lantern centerpiece. He wore a pair of sheepskin slippers, navy sweatpants, and a white long underwear top that bunched up on his belly.

Delma stood in front of the Wedgewood stove, her mane of gray hair hanging halfway down the back of her ankle-length red nightgown as she heaped sausage gravy onto a plate of grape-jellied biscuits. She spooned scrambled eggs next to the biscuits and laid four strips of bacon on top of the pile and set the plate down in front of William Robert.

"Where you thinkin' about headin' today?" she said.

"Thought I'd go over by Devil's Gap. There's some good bluffs back in there by Blackwater Holler. Back in there where Larry Dixon shot that big buck last year."

"Ain't that state ground?"

"Yeah, but nobody ever goes back in there 'cept hunters. I never seen no game wardens back in there."

"You goin' by yourself?"

"Yeah," William Robert said around a mouthful of eggs. "Couldn't get nobody to go with me. Brother Hiram's working a job down in Weeblow and Brother Jake don't have no gas money to drive up here. I prayed on it though, and the weather's supposed to be alright."

Delma furrowed her brow. Her tired gray eyes became pointed and serious, the plum-colored bags below darkening with worry. "You be careful then," she said. "Don't be handlin' none of them serpents outside of church neither, not when you ain't anointed."

William Robert smiled and wiped his hands on his shirt. "I'm in God's hands mama."

"I know that," she said."But so was your daddy."

He looked up at her. Soft yellow light and shadows danced over the lines and dents and tiny grey hairs on her face, and suddenly he knew what she would look like when she was a very old woman. "You ought not to say those things," he said quietly.

Delma turned to the floor and raised her faded eyebrows. "I know that. Do you have enough serpents for tonight's service if you don't catch any today?"

"I could make do, but I'm hurtin' for rattlers. I got some copperheads and a few cottonmouths, and I know I can find me some copperheads up on Mr. Jenkin's property. He's got some old plywood and tin layin' around back in the woods, but the only thing I ever caught back there was black snakes and copperheads."

"Well, you just be careful out there Robert. You comin' back home before service?"

He grinned as he stood up. She was the only one who still called him Robert. To everyone else he was Billy-Bob, or Pastor, or Pastor Billy-Bob. "Yes ma'am," he said.

"Alright. You got any idea when you'll be in?"

"Sometime before five I reckon."

Delma nodded gravely. She picked up William Robert's plate and trundled to the sink to do the washing, and William Robert yawned and stood up and went to the washroom. He shaved and brushed his teeth and went to his room and exchanged his blue sweatpants for a pair of Key overalls strapped loosely over his white undershirt, exchanged his fleece-lined moccasins for a pair of brown leather Chippewa snake boots. He kissed Delma goodbye before he left.

The sun was white in the tops of the trees. The sky was hard cobalt and the mist was gone. A gentle breeze cooled his face as he walked along the dirt path that led from the porch to the gravel drive by the white shed where his 1986 Ford F-150 was parked. It was two-tone blue, with thirty-two inch Mickey-Thompson tires and rust in the fender wells and floorboards. He tossed his tools in the bed and climbed inside and turned the key. The 302 barked through the glasspacks.

He backed into the soggy side yard and pulled out onto Hell's Bend Road, the lugs of his tires kicking gravel and heavy clods of red clay into his fenders as he weaved down the gently sloping spine of the mountain. When he reached Highway J he turned right and pressed the accelerator to the floor, and soon the whine of the tires drowned out the Ricky Skaggs tune crackling through the Ford's blown-out speakers.

It had been a wet fall in northern Arkansas and the ditches were full of muddy water and carp, and the bark of the flooded timber shone black in the sun. He turned left onto White Phantom Road and drove over the one-lane bridge. Blackwater Creek roiled below, its fudge-colored surface clogged with jagged wooden flotsam. The road turned to gravel on the far side of the bridge. It was narrow and cool and dark, shaded by hardwoods on both sides. William Robert bounced through the waterlogged chuckholes until he came to a nick in the timber. He turned right and drove up the dirt drive that led to a green knoll overlooking a small valley of swaying grass.

In the center of the knoll sat the prettiest little white country church you've ever seen.

He parked close and stepped down out of his truck, fumbled through his keys and unlocked the front door and walked into His Holiness Tabernacle Church of God. The air was still and slightly musty, and particles of floating dust glittered in the warm light spilling through the rectangular windows. There were five rows of pews on either side of the aisle, and at the front of the church was a short stage with a microphone stand in the center space normally reserved for a pulpit. Later in the evening, around six or so, William Robert would set up a folding table in front of the stage. He would cover it with a white cloth and bottles of strychnine and pine boxes filled with venomous snakes from the hills of Arkansas, and then Brother Hiram Walker would set up his keyboard and Brother Jerome Walker would strap on his electric Fender, and William Robert would take center stage in his light gray Western-cut suit and turquoise bolo tie. From there he would lead his small congregation in praise and song. They would dance to the old hymns, and they would speak unintelligible words and take up serpents and drink poison without fear, just as God commanded in the Book of Mark: Chapter 16, verse 18.

Behind the stage, on the left hand side of the building, was the door that led to the snake room. It was small and stuffy and hot, and it smelled like snake musk and aspen mulch. Homemade two-by-four tables held glass aquariums full of emaciated vipers. They lay coiled in beds of mulch, warming themselves under incandescent bulbs, pining away their days until they died and were disposed of like outdated props, their limp bodies tossed into the woods for the possums.

To the right of the door, leaning in the corner, was a homemade snake hook made from a golf club and a piece of cold-rolled steel, a long set of Pillstrom tongs William Robert had ordered from a Sportsman's Supply catalog, and a white five-gallon bucket with a screw-on lid. He took the tongs and the bucket and placed them into the bed of his truck, then continued north on White Phantom for another four miles. Turning right onto Buffalo Road at the base of Wolf Mountain, he passed a buckshot-pocked brown sign that said Devil's Gap 2 Miles.

The Devil's Gap trailhead was near the top of Wolf Mountain, tucked in a cedar-shaded corner of a small gravel parking area. William Robert parked in front of the sign. He stepped out and reached over the bedrail, picked up his tools and strode into the dense timber. The trail was well-worn and narrow, littered with brittle leaves that crunched underfoot, shattering like glass into tiny pieces to be reabsorbed by the ancient loam.

William Robert hiked slowly and carefully, using the tongs as a walking stick when he needed. He stopped at the half-mile marker and sat down to rest on a bench dedicated to Merle and Arlene Pemberton. The smell rising from the forest floor was sweet and spicy and dense, so fecund it was almost overwhelming. A gray squirrel peered down from a white oak and barked at him. A red-tailed hawk cried out overhead. A ladybug crawled onto the back of his hand from the armrest of the bench. He held his hand to his mouth and blew, and the ladybug spread her tiny black wings and buzzed away.

It was another half-mile to the twenty-foot tall pyres of sandstone that marked Devil's Gap. They appeared as unnatural as the travelers who passed between them, like decaying totems of a long-dead civilization. Their sides were streaked and water stained, and their compressed layers made them look like giant reams of wet, gray paper.

The trail arched upwards through the Gap, and soon the trees thinned and the sun shone brightly and William Robert was looking out over the expansive Blackwater Hollow. Sparse yellow grasses burst through cracks in the sandstone, and shortleaf pines grew tall and lean on the south facing plateau, chunky cones hanging in clusters from the tips of their branches.

A turkey buzzard soared high above the lush valley, its head glowing red in the late morning sun. William Robert watched it for a moment, and then he made his way towards the edge of the bluff where the loose rocks that attracted rattlers would be.

He stepped down onto a ledge that was dotted with jagged boulders and wild rose bushes, and there, on top of a flat piece of shale, lying in an S, was a timber rattlesnake. Its head was khaki colored, its body heavy and gray with velvet black chevrons flowing down its back. A flashy, rust-red stripe marked the spine, and at the tip of the tail was a rattle with eight perfect segments.

"Praise Jesus," William Robert said. He placed the bucket on the ground and walked carefully towards the snake. Using the tongs, he lifted it gently from the rock and carried it to the top of the plateau, away from any cracks or holes where it might escape, and laid it on the ground. The serpent seemed unaffected by the intrusion. It was quiet throughout, and simply tried to crawl away when it felt the cast aluminum jaws release their grip.

William Robert stared down, wonderment in his eyes as he watched the undulating creature that carried enough venom to kill ten men, yet seemed placid as a lamb. He felt his hands being guided downwards. "Praise Jesus," he whispered as his fingers touched the rough, dry keeled scales. His heart hammered in his throat as he lifted the snake from the ground. He raised it in front of his face, stared into the cold yellow eyes, and felt the Holy Spirit rumble through him like a peal of lightning. "Praise Jesus!" he shouted. He listened to God's praise echo through the hollow, and then he began to sing:

"Have you been to Jesus for the cleansing pow'r?" he cried, his feet stomping a jig into the rock. "Are you washed in the blood of th–"

A light smack on the right jaw interrupted the hymn. There was a prick of pain and an odd tugging sensation as the curved fangs tore free from the soft skin. William Robert heard a disconnected scream and a thud as the heavy viper hit the ground, and as he watched it crawl away lazily towards a bush honeysuckle, he touched his face in disbelief. He looked and saw that his fingers were painted with blood and clear yellow venom.

Almost immediately his lips and cheeks began to tingle. His mind went to Delma. He wondered if she was inside the little homestead where they had watched his father writhe and suffer and die. He felt scared and alone, but a part of him was thankful that only God and the mountain would bear witness. A tremulous heat race through him like a niacin flush, cold sweat boiling out as metallic bile rose in the back of his throat. Then a mechanical buzzing in his chest made it hard to breathe. His lungs quickly grew tired and his legs became heavy and weak. He found a fine smooth ledge overlooking the hollow and sat down.

A cool breeze rattled the leaves on the trees below. William Robert's eyelids grew heavy. It felt good to rest.

Merry Christmas Dooley Walker

Nathan Boone

Cass Calhoun turned off his headlights as he drove into the frozen grass on the side of Babar Road. The heavy steel body of his Mercury Eight flexed and groaned as he idled through a shallow ditch and into English Peuter's cut soybean field. The night was murky below a low layer of spongy gray clouds, and his eyes strained to see the weathered path that English's Allis-Chalmers had beaten into the dirt along the side of the field.

Droplets of sweat beaded on his forehead and fell down into his thick eyebrows, and soon the sedan's windshield was opaque with fog. He leaned forward in his seat and smeared a porthole in the glass with a flannel-covered forearm. A patch of moonlight showed through a break in the clouds, and in the white light the frosted bean stalks shined like metal bristles poking up from the hard black earth. The Mercury waded slowly through them, the flathead V-8 rumbling as stalks snapped like glass rods under the tires. In the rearview mirror he saw the row of pecan trees that bordered Babar fade into obscurity. He let his hands relax on the wheel. Now he was away from the prying eyes of passersby, safe in the righteous embrace of the night.

He hugged the hedgerow close, blackberry vines and honey locust branches with thorns like daggers scraping against the right side of the sedan, and soon a great stand of oaks materialized in the distance, their giant black trunks staggered like sentries before the steep, serpentine banks of the Jackdaw River.

Cass parked in the twisted, windblown grass in the corner of the field near a sinkhole filled with rusted appliances and engine blocks and scrap steel. He pulled on a pair of buckskin gloves and a wool stocking cap that was lying in the middle of the red and white bench seat, turned off the ignition, and stepped out. The air was cold and dry, and a stiff breeze was blowing through the field from the east. He looked back towards the road and felt the moisture leave his eyes. He squinted and blinked thick winter tears away and waited a moment longer. Then, when he was sure that no one was watching, he walked to the rear of the car.

The thin silver key slipped easily into place and the heavy lid opened with a thunk, and Cass lifted it and stared inside, plumes of vapor rising into his reddening face as he breathed.

Dooley's eyes were still open. They looked like the eyes of a catfish after he's laid in the bottom of the boat for a few hours. The whites were wrinkled and leathery, the irises muddy gray where they had been blue, and the stillness of the light standing on the pupils only served to lend credence to his condition: he was dead alright—a black, perfectly round .22 caliber hole bored into the skull above the right eye.

His face was simple and square and brutish, as if it had been shaped with a sledgehammer. He had oversized ears and hair that was styled into a greasy black pompadour, errant strands flipped down onto a vast, protruding forehead. His heavy jaw hung agape, showing crooked yellow teeth through pale lips that seemed to be frozen in a sneer.

Cass reached in and took hold of the blue denim shirt by the lapels, lifting the stiffening torso just enough to get his hands under the armpits. He clasped his hands around Dooley's chest and walked backwards. It was called the "cradle drop drag." He had learned it in the Marines, had employed it on several occasions in Guadalcanal and Tarawa and Tinian.

His forearms and biceps and back burned as he dragged the two hundred or so pounds of dead weight over the hard dirt at the field's edge, through weeds like tangled wire, then into the inky darkness of the forest. He was halfway to the river and his lungs were bursting with fire, his heart like a jackhammer pounding against the wall of his chest. He dropped the body and leaned against the rough trunk of a nearby tree, gulping at air that moved over his throat like steel wool. He pulled his stocking cap off and crushed it in his hand, felt the chill sink into his wet brown hair.

A whitetail deer snorted and broke through the timber; then another, and another, their hoof beats like the frenetic pounding of infantry boots. Behind him Cass could hear jagged chunks of river ice crashing into one another. They made eerie popping sounds, like the snapping of sinew. The winter air seemed to amplify the sounds and he felt himself tumbling into the blackness of his mind. In there he could hear the screams and howls of dying men and machine-gun bullets and mortars shells whistling overhead, and he could smell the sweetness, the rot, and the acrid cordite that settled heavy and deep in the lungs. He felt a lump like an apple rise in his throat, felt his sinuses swelling shut and clawed at the neck of his white undershirt in a panic. He couldn't breathe. His eyes filled with water and his cheeks peeled back and quivered.

He slapped himself hard. Then he looked up, out of habit, to see if anyone had seen him.

There was only Dooley, his own thousand yard stare gazing upwards into distant eternities.

Cass stretched his hat over his ears, scrubbed his face with his hands, and carried on, backwards through the trees to the edge of the steep bank that dropped down into a deep outside bend of the river. He left the body and walked back to the Mercury's trunk, pulled the heavy log chain out, and dragged it back. Kneeling down on the cold ground, he began to wrap Dooley up, starting at the boots that were covered in wet sawdust, cinching the chain tight with each revolution, up over the dark trousers and thick legs, over the barrel chest and broad shoulders, until the last coil choked the neck like an iron snake. He secured the chain with a padlock and stood up.

Here the river was wide and slow moving, black as crude oil with ripples and swirling currents that reflected moonlight like polished chrome. Cass breathed deeply and shoved the heavy corpse over the ledge with the heel of his boot.

"Merry Christmas Dooley Walker," he said, and watched as the water parted with a loud splash, frigid spray rising up six feet to touch his forehead. Dooley landed facedown. He seemed to float for a moment, and then he was gone, embraced by the river as readily and gently as if he were one of her own. The waves settled and in the darkness the water looked like wrinkled paint, then a plank of ice flowed over the spot and Cass turned away.

He walked back to the car and drove through the field, stopping once to let a vehicle pass, and then he eased out onto Babar and drove north over rough, washboard gravel. The air in the car had grown warm and stale and he was burning under layers of wool and cotton. He could smell the sourness of his sweat. He cracked his window and breathed. The air was cold and smooth, and it sparked his senses like a shot of good bourbon whiskey. It smelled of wood smoke and manure and sawdust and coal oil as he drove into the little town of Locklin, Missouri.

It was logging season, and the clapboard buildings on either side of the street were bursting with the migratory roughnecks—mostly hillbillies with small heads and big hands and Scandinavians with marble eyes and mustaches like nicotine-stained paintbrushes—who came to the fertile hills of the Ozarks each winter, forfeiting their holidays and their families (if they had any) in exchange for guaranteed work and a living wage, and a steady supply of your standard mill-town recreation.

They spent their days felling old growth, then at dusk they came into town on a string, filing into the tavern at the corner of Babar and Persimmon like cattle. Cass drove slowly past; saw their hulking silhouettes in the yellow lamp-lighted windows and through the front door that swung loosely on sagging hinges. As he turned right onto Persimmon, he watched a young, very tall man duck into the tin-walled whorehouse behind the tavern. A heavyset gypsy girl stood out front smoking. Cass lifted his fingers from the steering wheel and the girl waved lazily, her glowing cigarette cutting through the night like neon.

A mile past the tavern, at the base of Coulee's Peak—the second tallest summit in the Battle Hymn Mountains and highest point in Wyatt County—was Locklin Millworks. The building looked like an open-air tobacco barn, with rough-hewn uprights and sun-faded, triangular trusses strung with incandescent bulbs that burned the same color as lightning bugs in July. Third shift was still hard at it, and as Cass passed by he heard the big circular blade slice through an oak log. It made a high shrieking sound, like the death wail of a banshee echoing through the dark hills.

He rolled up his window and drove on, over a steep hill and down into Chinkapin Hollow. In the headlights the one-lane bridge looked rickety, with tall, spindly trestles like rust-colored grasshopper legs and a deck made of warped wooden planks that creaked and groaned under the weight of the Mercury. He stopped in the center of the bridge, and when he stepped out he could hear Chinkapin Creek roiling twenty feet below. It sounded like millions of feet all hurriedly shuffling in the same direction. He pulled the little Ruger revolver out of his coat pocket and tossed it into the water. It landed with a plop.

The road twisted upwards into the Battle Hymns, and soon he was winding around blind corners and switchbacks that clung like goats to steep cliff-sides, down again into John's Mule hollow, where he lived on a ten acre piece of ground passed down to him by his father.

His driveway was narrow and dark, red dirt and river rock crowded by thick tangles of grapevine and honeysuckle. His home—a small, red two-bedroom cottage with white shutters and a rust-streaked tin roof—was nestled in a half-acre clearing next to a garden patch and a dilapidated shed. He parked in front of the shed, next to his cruiser. It was a 1955 Chevrolet Bel Air coupe, gloss black with a white hood and white doors emblazoned with gold stars the size of turkey platters. "Sherriff" was painted above the stars in bold black letters.

Cass turned off the ignition and quietly stared out the windshield. The moon was full and bright overhead, the Milky Way a lacework of black dust and flame burning through sky the color of ocean water. He turned his eyes to the house. His tongue felt like leather between his teeth as he watched pastel gray smoke billow from the chimney. In his guts was the same churning trepidation he'd felt when he returned from the Pacific. Like an imposter, a wolf in civilian's clothing.

Then he opened the door.

He took the blood-stained canvas tarp from the Mercury's trunk, rolled it up and shoved it into the metal burn-barrel in the back yard; then he sneaked quietly through the back door into the mud-room and slipped off his boots. "Just me Lady," he whispered, reaching down to pat the wiggling Labrador's head. "Go on girl, go back to sleep."

Lady went to her pile of blankets in the corner as he eased the interior door open and stepped into the kitchen that still smelled of the ham supper they had eaten hours earlier. Half a sweet potato pie rested on the counter by the roll-top breadbox. Cass took a pint of Jim Beam from the pantry, a fork from the drawer next to the sink, and quickly cut the pie and the bottle down by a quarter each. When he was finished, he washed his fork and draped the cheesecloth back over the remaining pie, put the whiskey back in the pantry and walked down the hall, past framed photographs of war and peacetime, of wedding, birth, and childhood, to the first door on the left.

He opened the door slowly and crept in, his wool socks silent on the knotted pine floor. Betsy Mae lay sleeping on her twin mattress, the white and pink patchwork quilt pulled tight to her chin. Light from the hallway spilled over her strawberry hair and the bruises that shined red and purple, like daubs of jam on her face.

He walked over the white rug to her bedside, bent and kissed her forehead. She stirred and rolled to her side, and Cass took the little plush horse down from the window sill above the bed. It was nearly twenty years old, with fraying along the seams from so many long nights of watch duty. But it was there for her. And even if most of its stuffing had been ripped out, even if all that remained was an empty, ugly shell, like a blurry photographic reminder of lost innocence and foolish dreams, it always would be.

He held it for a moment, then touched its soft fur to Betsy Mae's hand. She whimpered as she grasped the horse and brought it to her breast. "Night Daddy," she whispered, cracking the eye that wasn't swollen shut.

"Night Punkin," he said. Her gold wedding band lay on top of the pink nightstand next to the bed. He took it with him as he left.

His bedroom was at the end of the hall. It was small and dark behind heavy curtains, with a white wrought-iron queen bed in the center and a white chest of drawers along the left wall beneath an oval mirror. He opened the top drawer and emptied his pockets, placing the ring, his keys, wallet, and folding Buck knife next to his deputy's badge and .38 service revolver. Then he undressed and crawled into bed.

Evelyn rolled to face him, her soft hand coming to rest on his cheek. His eyes had adjusted and he could make out the shape of her face, like a cherub with round cheekbones and big, dark eyes and full lips that smiled at his touch. "Everything go ok?" she said.

"Just fine."

She made a soft, pleased sound and scooted close. "I love you," she said, and pressed her lips hard against his.

"I love you too."

"Good," she said, and rolled to her back.

He was nearly asleep when he heard her say, "Darling?"

"Hmm?"

"What time is it?"

"Little after one."

"Merry Christmas."

"Merry Christmas."

ALONE

Emily Theroff

That spring they lived in the rock house, but they moved soon after to Delaware. Not the state, but a place on a creek named for the Delaware Indians. There had once been a small village where now, only a small clapboard house stood. This is what her husband, John, told her. He had grown up further along the holler and had told her stories of being a boy and remembering a store that also served as a post office. All she saw as evidence of a past settlement was a rock foundation that lay in tall weeds across the clay road from their place. She walked there in the cool of the morning as the mist rose off the creek's icy water. She crossed the road and climbed the rusted barbed-wire fence. She could be seen bending, then gently pulling the fresh grass from the old limestone rock, baring the rock to the sun. She would stand smoking, studying the rock formation as if perplexed by its existence. In the beginning she found it interesting, something to think about in the early hours of her day while their children slept peacefully.

Shortly after their move John, who often worked away, began spending more time gone from home. She often sat on the porch after work, staring past the patchy lawn of bluegrass to the field across the road. The evenings were long and her imagination was her best form of entertainment. She loved to read, and would sit on the gray board steps, reciting poetry from memory to the children. She would settle one of them between her knees and twirl the child's long hair around her fingers like spinning wool. As she completed this ritual, she gazed as if trying to glean something just beyond the field. Her attention was no longer fully with the children. One of the girls would beg, "My turn, Mama, my turn." She would return from vacancy, gently remove one child and replace it with the other.

Occasionally in the evenings she'd turn on the television with hope that through some act of divine providence, she might be able to make out a picture of some sort. A gray screen speckled in white was what she saw most often. A voice could barely be heard, a faraway sound of a voice. A voice calling out from the screen, one that could not fully reach her. They were too far away from anything, especially a television station. The children, watching their mother, heard only a sigh as she turned from her hope of adult communication. They were alone.

The evenings began to seem endless. After supper she washed dishes, then bathed the children. She gathered water from barrels that caught rainwater from the tin roof. She heated the water on the kitchen's blackened wood stove. She feared the mosquito larva she saw in the barrels, believing her children were in danger of catching polio. She endured the suffocating heat of the kitchen without complaint. She would splash herself with the cold drinking water from the artesian well near the house.

To the right of the house was a low-lying marshy area. She watched the mosquitos gathered there breeding, swarming as a gray fog in the summer's evenings. She came to hate the marsh, which felt as if it were an entity that held secrets and things to dread, disease and death. It was the greatest reminder of how alone they were, when John was away. Gradually the loneliness stayed, despite her husband's presence. The marsh had its own song, and the song had no end. The frogs began their call just after dusk, when the last of the day's promise slid behind the hill. She told herself the sun was still there, that somewhere in the world just over the hill it was shining brightly. This was in the beginning.

Now she no longer drew comfort from knowing the whereabouts of the sun. Longing to see it and its solace, she began to plan a way to catch just one more glimpse of it. She charted a course in her mind. When the sun lay low at the hilltop she would start her personal quest. First she would make sure the children were safe on the screened back porch. She would cross the creek at the shoal. The water ran fast there, though not enough to whisk her off her feet. Once across, she would maneuver the gentle bank slope to the line of small cedar trees. If need be, she would pull herself up by the tree trunks. Closer to the top, the terrain grew rocky with large limestone boulders jutting out of barren clay soil. She envisioned herself at the crest, viewing the sought-after sphere. In her mind it offered comfort and freedom from the valley of darkness that lay below.

One evening, after finishing her chores, she felt her skin was crawling. Looking at her arms, she saw nothing there. She began to pace the perimeter of the yard. Rubbing her arms as if to push away some unseen menace was of little comfort, so she scratched at her skin, leaving long reddened marks with blood at the surface. Her marching continued. As she passed the porch where the girls set playing she heard them scream and saw them pointing at her arms. Looking down,she then saw long bloody marks on both forearms. The girls ran to her and began to pull at her shirt. The tugging of her children helped draw her back, to comfort them, offering reassurance everything would be alright. She washed her arms and wrapped a tea towel around the traces of open wounds. She then put them to bed, whispering words of familiar stories and love to comfort each of them. They soon slept.

She knew she must try to reach the top of the hill. She splashed through the creek at the shoal. Slipping, then falling into the icy waters, she lay there allowing the cold water to relieve the sting she now felt in her arms. She lay belly down against the slippery cool rocks of the shoal. Face down, she slurped water with the dog that trailed after her. Soon she got to her feet and pushed on with her quest for the daylight. Struggling with the sharp incline, she made her way to the to the hill's top. There she stood and looked to the next hill. On the horizon, a faint glow of yellow could be seen. The world of her valley below the summit lay blanketed in darkness. Her sojourn, defeated.

The return to the little farm was a return to utter aloneness. She sensed the abyss just beyond the marsh with its whirring mosquitos and driven, singing frogs. "The loneliest place on earth," she whispered.

Alone in the dark, she watched watching across the yard, beyond to the field that held the rock foundation. She saw it as it was fifty years before. People came and went on horseback and in wagons. They collected their mail and traded for grocery staples. She saw them stop and talk to one another about the news contained in their letters. Good news, mediocre, and the bad. She sat for hours and watched the goings-on across the road. Watched until the lamp in the window was snuffed and the proprietor walked down the road toward home.

She rose, brushed her clothes and went inside.

Minecraft: The Ozarks Mod & Texture Pack

Marta Ferguson

Not much to do, really. Lummelunda,
old karst not far from Notch's own Stockholm,
clearly inspired the cave systems under
almost any Minecraft surface biome.
But giving it that Ozarks feel, let's see:
some stalactites in bright mineral hues,
some shale, that shaggy rock, in its many
paleo-grunge formulations,gray-blue.
Tiny forest-service wet-fracking crews,
bus-borne Branson tourists, heartbreaking signs
on chains to string across the best venues
for Ozarks bats: KEEP OUT WHITE NOSE SYNDROME.
Eyeless cave fish, rare hellbenders, darters,
whose only home may soon be on servers.

Rose O'Neill's *Sweet Monsters* Emerge from the Bonniebrook Woods, 1894

Marta Ferguson

Two wooded days to reach the rough cabin.
A darker, wilder place I've never known.
The wagon track more primitive each turn,
forest more dense, lesser light, greater shadow.

And I began to see the scene anew.
Its woodland souls stepped forth, great ropy limbs,
knobbled torsos, their eyes so deep I drew
my own away, to no avail. I penned

such images those days, *primeval shapes*,
their arching bodies rooted to the land
from which they grew. All boundaries erased,
wood-stone-wind-water-light creatures whose hands

grew large enough to cradle us, like babes
to breast, to soothe, nurture, entangle, save.

*Italics mark O'Neill's own words.

All Shook Up at the Branson Elvis® Festival* A Found Poem of Elvis® Song Titles

Marta Ferguson

Spring fever hits and fools rush in, to Branson:
Teddy bears, hound dogs, big hunks o' love.
Headed for Heartbreak Hotel (La Quinta)
to rip it up. Fools! Fools! Fools! Girls! Girls! Girls!

Can't help falling in love, by and by.
C'mon everybody, doncha' think it's time?
Enough hard luck, hard knocks. Good-time Charlie's
got the g.i. blues. I'm gonna sit right down

and cry. Ask me, are you lonesome tonight
at Dick Clark's American Bandstand Theater?
Do the vega, do the clam, do not disturb:
whole lotta shakin' going on, Ultimate

Elvis® Tribute Artist Contest™ in progress.
Release me to my happiness (Elvis®
Vendor Village, Elvis® Meet & Greet,
Elvis® Karaoke, always on my mind).

Could I fall in love, come what may, down by
the riverside, end of the road? Rock-A-Hula
Baby, let's play house. I'm almost always true.
You're gentle on my suspicious mind

and I'm stuck on you, softly and tenderly.
Any way you want me, that's how I will be,
puppet on a string, pocketful of rainbows.
Let it be me, let me be the one to topple

Elvis® Ben Thompson and Elvis® David Lee.
The bitter elvii are, the harder they fall.
Big love, big heartache. Jailhouse dixieland rock's
all that I am. Just call me lonesome, and ultimate.

*Unlike the contest it describes, this poem was not
sanctioned by Elvis® Presley Enterprises, Inc.

Blue Trillium

Rebecca Graves

It came to her where she was, who she was. The house, this house, must be her daughter's. Her daughter, Amanda. She remembered her. The house, while familiar, still seemed strange. Rose sat in an arm chair which faced the window. A goldfinch and a female cardinal shared a feeder. Two squirrels competed for another. A flock of sparrows hopped on the ground beneath.

Rose looked around. This was not her home, though she recognized the room. She knew the room she slept in was down the hall behind her. The living room opened to the kitchen with no wall between. Rose found that strange, as if the house were not finished. Beyond the kitchen was the laundry and the side door. She had been here before, she knew the house, but it wasn't home. It wasn't her house.

Rose turned and looked at the mantel over the stone fireplace. Pictures of Amanda with a man and a child. Rose waited and the name Phil came to mind. Yes, of course, Amanda's husband, and this must be their child. She stared at the girl in the photo but no name came for her. Rose smacked her hand on the arm of the chair, but still no name came.

Tears came and were a relief to her dry eyes. She remembered Amanda as a girl. Remembered her as a baby, when she herself was young. Rose remembered her own house, smaller than this one, the rooms properly closed off from one another, not all opening one into the next. She had no mantel, no fireplace, so had hung the family photos in the hall. The better place to put them. That way you didn't have to invite folks all the way into your house for them to see the joy and result of your life. Rose remembered the dining room and living room. She pictured her kitchen and the lilac bush outside the windows over the sink. Jack had planted the lilacs for her when they had moved in.

Jack, where was he? She looked around. No, this was not her house. It came to her that it was Amanda's house. Jack, he must be still at the shop. He would come and pick her up and they would go home. She would wait for him in the drive. No sense making him come all the way in. Jack. She smiled and thought of his thick, dirty-blond hair and the way he smiled at her when they were alone in the kitchen, the smell of lilacs drifting in through the window. She would make him a pie when they got home. No, too late in the day for a pie. A cake. Lemon is his favorite. She was sure she had lemons in the refrigerator, but best to have him stop at the Piggly Wiggly just to be certain.

Julia flopped backward onto her bed, her phone in hand, a bowl of ice cream on the nightstand. Grandma had been slumped in her chair, head forward in sleep, breathing deep and even when Julia checked on her a couple minutes ago. She reminded Julia of her cousin's baby, all fallen in on herself. Julia looked out the window—the sun was still up but only for an hour or so more. She looked at her watch and sighed. Her mom still had a couple hours left of her meeting. The home nurse had gone for the day, so Julia was left babysitting. She quick-dialed her friend Olivia and set the phone to speaker, then placed it on the bed and picked up the bowl of ice cream.

"Hey, Julia, what's happening?"

"Eating ice cream and babysitting Grandma. You?"

"Ooh, you know how to live. Rocking it with Grandma. I'm over at Gwen's baking cookies. You should come over."

"Can't. Mom won't be home for another hour."

"But it's summer vacation."

"Nope, she won't go out again. And Dad's out of town, so who would watch Grandma? Not like we can take her along. You know how she is."

"Yeah, that sucks. I'm never getting old. Not old like that."

"Me either. What are you doing tomorrow? Want to come by and swim?"

"Sure. Hey, Gwen and I were talking about that time in fifth grade you got us to believe that the ghost of the Blue Girl was real. Remember?"

"Yeah, I remember." Julia shifted on the bed.

"And, you got us all to hike up into the woods, even little Danny Howe."

"He's not so little anymore, have you seen him?"

Olivia laughed, "He was little then, and we all kept asking about the ghost, only there wasn't any ghost. And then, Gwen jumped out from a tree and everyone screamed. Even Danny, especially Danny. That was the best prank ever!"

Julia laughed, though she didn't feel it. She had thought the ghost was real. She remembered the laughter she heard in the woods and how the birds would circle around the girl when she called to them. She remembered how she and the girl would walk the woods together. But there had been nothing there. She had been wrong. There was no Blue Girl ghost. She prayed her friends never found out she believed it.

The conversation turned back to cookies and swimming and boys. The ice cream bowl sat empty on the nightstand and the screen of her phone cast more light than the window. "Bye. See you tomorrow," said Julia. She noticed the dusk out the window.

"Shit! Grandma!" Julia jumped up and ran from her room. The living room was empty. "Grandma!" she yelled. "Grandma!" Julia ran to Grandma's room. Empty. She ran throughout the house shouting "Grandma!" When she came to the kitchen and saw the side door wide open, Julia went cold. *Let her be in the garden, let her be in the garden,* she intoned to herself as she slipped on her sneakers.

Emmaline Blue drifted through the trees, the shimmer of her growing more visible in the fattening dusk than in the daytime sun. So many years she had spent in these woods, and before that in the pasture lands they once had been, pasture cleared by her father and grandfather. Her soul ached to see them again: her grandfather, her parents, and especially her sister Nora. The setting of the sun set the woods alive with light and life. At the woodland's edge the sparrows and finches foraged, then flocked, then fell out to forage again before the sun sunk low enough to take its light with it.

Emmaline moved from the woods into the field beyond and listened to the rustling of the mice in the roots of the grasses and coneflowers. She watched the sun slip to the seam of the horizon. A flock of goldfinches flew overhead and Emmaline flung out her arms and spun. The movement, the flutter of the spin was pure joy. Head tipped back, eyes closed, lips in a smile, Emmaline whirled among the flowers and the birds wheeled around her.

When she stilled, an old woman was standing in front of her. The woman clapped her hands together and whispered, "Emmaline!" Emmaline faltered, wavered in her brightness. "Don't go," the woman said in a papery voice. "Don't go. We can pick primrose together and milkweed." The woman's white hair stood in wisps around her head. Emmaline did not know her.

She had picked flowers with many girls over the years, but knew no old woman.

The woman's face lost its light. "You don't remember me. You don't remember your Rose."

Emmaline thought of milkweed pods and primrose blossoms; she thought of a girl with chestnut hair and home-sewn dresses, a girl named Rose. She brightened and spun in a circle around Rose, who laughed and clapped. "Emmaline! Emmaline!" she chanted in her thin voice. They walked through the field and Rose picked smooth beard-tongue and coneflower. Her stiff fingers could not work them into wreaths, but dropped them instead. Laughing, Rose picked another and patted it onto her head.

Twilight wrapped around them. Rose's knees ached. "I don't know where home is. Where is home?" Emmaline shook her head. Rose pressed her fingertips to her lips. "Jack was supposed to come get me. Where is Jack?"

Outside, evening birds sang from the oak tree. Julia found no trace of Grandma, not in the garage, nor the garden, nor the shed where her dad kept the mower. She pulled out her phone and called her mom. At the sound of her mother's voice, Julia broke, tears rolling down her cheeks. "Mom." Her voice was a whisper. "I'm sorry Mom, Grandma got out. I can't find her. I'm sorry. I'm sorry." She shut her eyes and listened to her Mom, taking her anger as a penance. "I'm sorry, Mom, I'm so sorry." Her mom had hung up before Julia finished.

Julia wiped her eyes with the heels of her hands. With shaky fingers, she dialed the neighbors. "Mrs. Geier? This is Julia, Julia Baum. My Grandma has gotten… wandered off. Could you keep an eye out for her?" Julia held the phone to her ear. "Yes… yes, my mom's on her way home… no, Dad's out of town… Thanks,

Mrs. Geier." Julia walked again around the yard and back through the house, only to confirm she was alone. She went back out the side door and stood biting her lip. Where would she have gone? Where?

Julia followed the long drive to the road. She paused at the mailbox. No shuffling shapes either way. Crickets sang among the tickseed. Julia turned left and walked along the road. The sun had passed the horizon but still cast light enough to see. Civil twilight, her dad had called it. She wished she'd grabbed a flashlight. She scanned the road, the ditches, the fields, but what if Grandma had fallen? How would she see her? She called out, "Grandma! Grandma! Where are you? Grandma!" Only the crickets answered.

In the distance, headlights glanced off the road. Julia hoped and feared that it was her mother. She headed out towards the woods. The light shifted. No, she thought, I have to find her. The shadows grew together, darkened. Julia heard a car door slam in the distance. Heard her mother's voice calling out, "Mom! Rose!" Julia continued on toward to the woods, stumbling in the weeds. There a light flickered. Probably Mom's flashlight. Julia paused. The light flickered, like fireflies. Julia walked on but the light pulled at her. It moved, turned. She started, then ran towards it.

There, in the center of a circle of light, stood her grandma. "Grandma!" Julia hurried toward her. She watched the fireflies circle so like the birds she remembered. "Emmaline," she whispered. Grandma Rose stood alone, and turned to Julia. "Who are you? Do you know Jack? He's supposed to come get me."

Her Men

Rebecca Graves

The old dog paced the pasture trail ahead of Rivka, his paws kicking up puffs of dust. Torque, her son Rick had named him. A half-smile twisted Rivka's mouth. Not much torque left in him now. Every so many paces he stumbled over a rut or a root. Rivka winced to see it. Age, she thought, catches us all. All but my bright, my beautiful boy Rick, Rick who should be here now walking with his dog and a child of his own. There was no profit in thoughts such as these, and she chided herself. She pushed her steps a bit faster.

Summer was tired this year, brown and brittle. Worn out from weeks of 100 degrees and no rain. She turned her back on the cracked pasture and headed for the drab leaves of the woods. Torque doubled back and caught up with her on the path that wandered to the creek.

The farm had been in her family for generations. She and her husband, John, had worked it since their wedding day. Her men, she called them, John and Rick. Rick a leaner, taller version of his father. She pictured them cutting hay, John in the cab and Rick on the wagon, sweaty and covered in chaff. In the morning Kenny, from a couple of farms over, was coming to slaughter her last few cows. By this time tomorrow there would only be Rivka and Torque and a handful of chickens.

Baking John's and Rick's favorite cakes on their birthdays and taking the cakes to their graves was her one indulgence to her grief. Other women yammered about their children having moved away and never bothering to call. Sometimes, Rivka wanted to shake them, yell at them. At least their seed was somewhere growing. All of hers were buried in the dead soil.

Dusk crept in from the edges of the east and still the sweat trickled down her temples, her spine, and from under her breasts. Even the sparrows on the branches panted. Only the cicadas sang, joyous in the heat. Though fall was weeks away, leaves covered the path, crisp under their steps.

She walked out from the woods to the bank of the creek, stopped and scanned the bed. Rocks and tree snags jutted up dry and sharp like old bones. She walked straight out to the center of the bed, turned right and walked up the creek, seeking out any remaining pools of water. It was several yards before she found one. She stood and watched the minnows panic in the shallows like horses in a burning barn.

Torque trotted along the low ridge, then stopped, ears cocked forward. His eyes looked to see what his nose had found. Rivka glanced up and smiled at Torque, who tensed, then pounced. An orange striped ribbonsnake whipped out from the scrub and wound down the bank toward the creek. Torque jumped down after it.

The rocks shifted and slid from under his paws. Torque skidded and rolled down with them. His yelp blended with their clattering. The tumble of dog and rock came to rest in the creek bed. Time hung for a moment. Even the cicadas paused their drone.

Torque pushed himself up, failed and fell. The smile drained from Rivka's lips and she scrambled over the stones to where he lay. He lifted his head at her approach, tried again to stand, only to fall. Rivka squatted next to him and he met her eyes with his. She rubbed his head, the velvet of his ears, and his tail thumped against the rocks. She murmured sounds to him as she ran her hands down his right front leg. Torque whimpered at her touch. Her fingers found a break in the bone. Rivka's breath caught in her throat.

"Ah, Torque, what am I going to do with you? You can't walk with a broken leg." His eyes stared into hers. He reached his neck forward and licked her face. Rivka sighed. She shifted her position, slowly worked her arms under him and hefted his 60 pounds. Torque whined and twisted his head towards her. His tongue licked the air.

Rivka carried him back along the path. The cicadas droned louder. To Rivka, their call to mate was the sound of the sweat, the heat, the hard hard walk of living. An ache kindled in the small of her back. Her arms shook and her sweat dripped from her eyebrows into her eyes.

She reached the farmhouse and stumbled on the steps up to the side porch, which held a pair of sturdy wooden chairs and a bed for Torque. They had never used the real front entrance. It had long been hidden from view by overgrown yews that John had never gotten around to cutting down. Rivka knelt on the worn wooden boards of the porch and laid Torque on his bed.

She sat back on her heels and wiped the sweat from her eyes, then reached over and picked up the water bowl and held it up to Torque. He lapped at the water once, twice as if to please her. Rivka set the bowl back down. She reached out her hand and petted his head, scratched the ruff of his neck. "The vet is closed this late in the day or I would take you there," she said. "The university clinic would be open. But we don't have that kind of money. What do you think, Torque?" She moved her hand from his head to his leg. It was swollen, hot to the touch. He lowered his head and licked her hand.

Rivka shook her head. "We can't leave that for a day or two, can we boy?" His tail thumped the wood boards. She pressed her lips together, thought of the balance in her bank account.

She heard John's voice in her head. *Torque is old and a dog*. She closed her eyes and pictured the day of Rick's thirtieth birthday when John, grinning, walked into the dinner party with a puppy squirming in his arms and set it on Rick's lap.

Torque whined. His tail was still and his head was heavy in her lap. Rivka let her tears fall, stroked his head, his ears, his sides. She forced herself up and walked from the porch into the kitchen. She took her .22 from the rack, filled the chamber. Her lips trembled. She could afford a bullet.

She walked back out to Torque and crouched down next to him. "You go find those two men. And, you tell them that I love them, you hear me. But first, you and me, Torque…you and me, we'll go on one more hunting trip." Torque's eyes were bright with pain. Rivka stood, the gun ready at her side. She pulled a treat from her pocket and tossed it into the yard. His eyes followed its arc. The crack of the shot echoed off the barn and into the fields. As the echoes died, Rivka heard the cicadas humming in the heat.

Low Water Crossing

Bridget Bufford

Ashley leans against the fender of her Chevy S-10, cradling a mug of coffee. The aroma washes her face. Rays of sun press the mist downhill, back to the creek. Fletcher just called, and he sounds excited. Either he's finally putting together his fish tank, or his little brother Turnip has come for a visit.

Turnip, whose real name is Eugene, is an honest-to-God genius. He could have studied engineering at Washington University in St. Louis, but instead took a scholarship at Rolla. Fletcher's been lonesome for him.

She gets in and tries the truck again. The starter clicks. She can hear Fletcher's Camaro drop a gear and climb. He's cresting the hill, in a good mood for once, and the damn truck's dead. Ashley opens the hood.

Fletcher parks away from the drive. His face falls. "Won't start?"

With a screwdriver Ashley pries the leads from the battery, then opens the cells. "Well, there's part of it."

"I can jump it," Fletcher offers.

"Wait till I get water in her. I think Mama's got some distilled she uses in the iron."

Fletcher collects the jumper cables and his work gloves. The screen door bangs. Ashley hands him a warm can of Coke to pour over the terminals. Flakes of corrosion peel away on the foam. Ashley rinses the battery from a plastic jug, then adds water to each cell. "Lucky I checked," she notes. "Might of exploded if we'd put cables on it."

Fletcher bites his lip. Their eyes meet.

Ashley's mother brings out a paper bag. "Y'all take this down to Ray once you get going," she says, and Ashley nods.

Fletcher pulls up the Camaro. "I used to like Ray," Ashley says. "He seemed like a steady guy. I guess you never know."

"He don't look right." Fletcher starts his car, and Ashley hits the truck ignition. After a slow grind, it catches. "Let her run a minute," Fletcher says, and puts his gloves and lunch into the truck.

"Well, he's drunk as Cooter Brown, and never eats except somebody brings something. You wouldn't look right, either."

"Who's Cooter Brown?"

"Some old boy stayed shit-faced through the Civil War," Ashley says.

Fletcher parks back in the yard. The Camaro is powerful but low-slung, prone to banging the undercarriage on rocks. Chick magnet, though it won't haul anything. Ashley tells her mom they're leaving.

"Where we headed?" Ashley asks, though she has a suspicion. Ever since his spring haircut, when he found a copy of *Mother Earth News* among the *Missouri Conservationist* and *Field & Stream*, Fletcher has been talking about backyard aquaponics. Day before yesterday, he borrowed the S-10 to haul off debris from a remodeling job.

"That job last week had an old fountain. I salvaged some pipe and a pump, and half a tube of silicone sealant. Now all I need's a pallet tote." He fishes out his crumpled magazine pages. "How many of those do you see just piled up behind somebody's barn? Course it has to be food grade storage; you don't want something that's going to kill all your fish. Take citric acid.

People eat it all the time. But even if you wash your tank out, it'll kill fish dead. You want a good clean tote. Food grade from a prison would be just right."

"Nearest prison's Jefferson City," Ashley says.

"I'm not trusting this truck to get us to Jeff," Fletcher says. "But there's totes on damn near every farm. Sometimes they call them IBC tanks."

"I know what they are." Ashley shifts down, turning off the hard road. "But nobody's going to waste a good tank. They use them for rain barrels, or mix up Roundup inside 'em."

"Not everybody," Fletcher says. "Old man Royce got all them horses. He mixes his own sweet feed for the mares and foals."

Ashley parks beside the creek. "So?"

"Molasses!" he says, and grins. Ashley grins back; she can't help it. She and Fletcher have been friends since grade school. "You and me are going to pick pumpkins," he continues, "and his late squash, and he's going to give me a pallet tote."

A blue heron breaks from the mist and circles the low-water crossing, near enough that they can hear its wings. "Ray?" Ashley calls. "Yo, Ray?"

No answer. Fletcher says, "You suppose he's dead?"

"Maybe he's sleeping." They stare toward his tent, but they both know he no longer sleeps. Ray is a Critchfield, same as Ashley's mother. Until last summer, he drove the delivery truck for a feed store. Now he lives by the creek, telling his story to anyone who comes around.

Gravel shifts off the far bank. Ray heaves himself up from a deadfall. His bottle has only a swallow left. "You boys," he begins. He stumbles into the creek, missing nearly every stone set there for crossing. "I've been drunk for thirty-one days." He's been saying that all summer.

"Brought you some food." Ashley takes out the grease-stained sack from the front seat. "Chicken Mama made, and her potato salad. You always liked her potato salad, Ray."

"Ash?" Ray is bone-thin and burned to peeling. "Thought you was a fella."

"Happens." She puts her hands in the pockets of her Carhartts.

"You're Turnip's brother," he says to Fletcher. "Where's Turnip?"

"College." Fletcher shakes his head. "Sure do miss him."

He could have smacked his own mouth once the words were out of it. Back in July, Ray's youngest boy welded a pipe bomb, then went to test it in an old chest freezer. Nothing happened. After a few minutes, Billy jerked open the door to check the fuse. Pieces of him still stain the rusted cars and microwaves of the backyard Ray avoids. He was the same age as Turnip.

Turnip will be home at Thanksgiving. Billy isn't ever coming home.

"I know you do," Ray says. "Him and Billy were in the same class." He sets his food on a stump, near the ashes of a dead fire. Ashley rummages behind the passenger's seat, then sets a couple jug lines near a brushy part of the bank. "Have you a catfish later on," she says. "You need to eat."

Fletcher crouches at the bank. Three trout dart past like liquid silver. Ray's unsteady feet spurn gravel, then he clutches Fletcher's shoulder. "Them's good eatin'," he observes. "I've been drunk for...um..." He sucks a chicken bone.

Under Ray's grasp, Fletcher's skin crawls. He clears his throat. "You'd think a trout can't live in a tank," he says. "I read that they do okay if you keep them cool, and they have a good conversion rate. Means they grow fast on what food you give 'em." He looks up at Ray. The older man's eyes judder, and he takes a cross-legged step. All that rock; that water. "But how you gonna keep 'em cold? Unless you set up in a cave. A few perch or little bass, they'll do just fine. You can keep a fish in three gallons of water, once the bio filter gets established."

Ashley takes a trash bag from the truck. "Help me out, Fletcher." They pick up tuna cans, half-pint bottles, soggy paper bags. "Ray, you oughtn't throw your trash around like this. Mama sent some black bags, and I want you to start using them. Next time I come, I'll haul them off. This crossing don't belong to you. Families come here to swim and picnic. Nobody wants to see your garbage."

"Where does he get his whisky?" Fletcher mutters.

Ashley straightens. "Somebody brings it. Don't know if they aim to do a kindness, or what."

"Yeah." Fletcher ties off the bag and slings it into the pickup. He draws out a pack of cigarettes, takes three for himself and gives the rest to Ray. "Let's go. Them pumpkins are waiting."

"Ray, you check them jug lines." Ashley crawls the Chevy across the spillway. "I hate to pick squash. Or pumpkins. Or cucumbers. "

"At least a squash is a meal. A Hubbard, or even a pumpkin. What are you going to do with a cucumber?" Fletcher slings an arm out the window. "But they all give me rashy wrists. Even with gloves on, they get up on your skin."

"I brought gloves," Ashley says. "Ray. Goddamn. "

"I know," Fletcher says. "I hope I never have kids. Turnip ought to have some, but not me."

At Royce's place they each take a tarp and a curved knife, then roll down their sleeves and get to work.

"I got a stock tank from my uncle." Fletcher takes a dip of Copenhagen, then offers the tin. "It leaks, but as long as I top it off every few days, I can keep some starter fish."

"Why do you need a pallet tote if you got a stock tank?" Ashley wipes a sleeve across her forehead. "Just use that."

"Won't work. You need to be able to set up a tray for your plants, so that you can flood and drain them and run the water back into the tank. Stock tank's got nothing to latch onto it. I'd need to put in a stand pipe, a submersible pump... all of that."

"You could do that on the tank just as well."

"No, I could not." Fletcher heaves up an especially large pumpkin, totters backward and catches his heel on another.

Ashley grabs his arm. "Don't get pissy, Fletcher."

"Son of a bitch probably weighs sixty pounds." Fletcher rolls it onto the tarp. "Peter Pumpkin Eater and his wife could fit into that one. Anyway, the thing about a pallet tote is that you cut eight inches off the top of it, flip that part over and it sets right into the bottom. That holds your plants—your spinach and collards, whatever you want. Doesn't have to be greens, but they fit in there good. Just drill through it for the plumbing and the drainage. Fish on the bottom, greens on the top. You get a couple of those going, so that you got your breeder fish and the ones you're gonna net and eat, and a man could live on that. Shoot a deer in the fall, grow some taters, trade fish for anything else you want. It's a perfect design. It's... it's elegant."

Ashley bawls out a laugh. "Elegant? I damn near dropped my pumpkin. You crazy bastard."

"That's what the magazine called it. An elegant solution."

"To what? Your elegant problems?"

"Shut up."

"For real, though," Ashley says. "You know who you sound like?"

They say it together: "Turnip."

"I bet you miss him. Is he going to help you?"

"I might not be a genius, but I can plumb a fish tank." Fletcher grabs one side of the tarp and gestures to the other. Pumpkins roll around crazily as they pull them to the truck. "But there's something about it... about backyard aquaponics..." He looks away.

"Sorta makes you feel like he's around?" Ashley asks.

"Turnip's always been...well, you know. He's my little brother. It's different with him gone. I just gotta make the best of it."

They finish stacking the pumpkins on the flatbed. Bud Royce has already loaded the tote onto Ashley's pickup. He gives them each $30 besides, and a couple of big yellow squash. Fletcher stares up at his prize. "Look at that. Damn. Finally."

They stop by the grocery for some beer. Fletcher's in such a good mood that he agrees to go check on Ray again before bringing the tote home. He even gets bacon and some paper plates.

At the crossing, Ray already has a fire going. "Hey, fellas," he says, then squints at Fletcher. "You say you miss Turnip?'

"Sure." Fletcher shifts uneasily. "Let me get you some more wood."

The jug lines snared two good-sized catfish. Ashley skins and guts them while Fletcher cooks the squash with bacon, then fries up the rest of it for grease. Ray cracks open a beer. "I been drunk for thirty-one days," he says. He stares again at Fletcher. "You think you don't know, but you know," he says.

"Let's get some food in you, old man." Ashley slips the fillets into the pan, flinching back from the spatters. "This is going to cook real fast. You got salt and pepper, don't you?"

Fletcher sets out the plates and forks. Ray finishes his beer. "You think you don't know," he says again, and disappears into his tent. He comes back out with a rifle, using it like a walking stick to steady himself.

"Whoa, whoa," Ashley says. "Set that down and come eat, Ray. We got this nice catfish and squash. Smells real good."

Ray places the gun behind his stump and produces cardboard shakers from his pocket. Ashley seasons the fish. It isn't much for three of them, but there's a blue ton of squash. Fletcher peppers it liberally, then divides it on the plates. Ray brings out a box of saltines to share.

Fletcher piles squash onto a cracker and crumbles bacon on top. "Pumpkin pickin' made me hungry," he says. "I wish I had a bucket. We could net some perch."

"Billy," Ray says. He opens a beer and drinks it down, then wipes a hand across his mouth.

Ashley sips her own beer; she'll only have the one, since she's driving. "This is real good," she says. "Take my bacon, Ray. I got plenty."

"You think you don't know." Ray pokes a finger at Fletcher. "You know. You damn well know."

"For Christ's sake, Ray. I'm trying to eat. What the hell is it that I'm supposed to know?"

"Billy wasn't ever smart enough to make a bomb on his own," Ray says. "Billy wasn't smart at all."

Fletcher sighs. He scrapes up his last mouthful of bacon and squash, then tosses the plate into the fire. "Billy is dead, Ray. You shouldn't talk about him like that." He begins to walk toward the truck. "Come on, Ashley. Been a long day."

"Let me just wash up." Ashley takes the skillet and knife to the creek, and drops them both when she hears the shot. The report echoes from the bluff. She wants to turn around but she can't. Not until the gun fires again.

Fletcher is on his knees, hands clasped over his head. Ashley runs to him. Her ears ring.

"There you go." Ray throws down the rifle and starts to cry. "I know you know," he says again.

Fletcher trembles, but seems okay. "The son of a bitch," he whispers.

Ashley looks him over. Fletcher points to the back of the pickup. The pallet tote has two holes punched through the near side, gaping tears opposite. Fletcher collapses against Ashley, who steadies him. "One good thing," Fletcher says. "Just wanted one decent thing in my life."

He stands taller, then shakes his head. "Leave the beer," Ashley says, and drives them away.

1,000 Miles

Bridget Bufford

Dr. Kenneth Cooper changed my life. Dr. Cooper is the father of the fitness revolution. In 1975, my junior year of high school, he wrote a book called *Aerobics*, and it was not about women in leotards jumping around to dance music. *Aerobics* was serious science, a way of quantifying cardiovascular exercise so that an athlete could track her progress—running, swimming, riding a bike—just as easily as a weightlifter could count the next ten pounds he added to his bench press.

I devoured that book. I studied the charts and conversions, I memorized the physiology of oxygen uptake, I learned the importance of duration vs. rate of activity performed. It was beautiful, it was inspirational; it all made sense.

I was so impassioned by the book that I even, for a short time, tried to run. I am stocky, with stumpy little legs—your average softball body. For motivation, I recruited my best friend Corey. She was a much better runner than me, but once the school year got going, she lost interest, for which I was grateful. I continued to memorize Dr. Cooper's book and decided I would be an exercise physiologist.

That time, on the verge of senior year, comes back to me as a series of impressions: the taste of a McDonald's vanilla shake; the creak of a tail gate lowered for a bench; the bump and groan of truck springs as our butts landed on that tail gate. Nothing complete; each image is separate, without connections. The smell of the liniment Corey used, a greasy trail of it on her shins, her thumbs pressing into sore, smooth flesh. No Corey in my mind, just a tanned shin, rough knuckly hands, a dirty sneaker with laces gone gray.

Senior year was going to be great. Everybody said it would be, as if repetition alone would make it so. The sophomores and freshmen envied us; our parents envied us more. That I remember: "Make the most of this year, kid. You're on top of the world." We were at some uneasy place, for sure.

Another memory: Corey's announcement in the locker room. "Linda," she said, "I'm not playing softball this year." It was early spring, almost the end of junior year. Corey sat on the long bench, one foot braced against the locker; she was tying an Adidas running shoe, stiff and new.

My left hand gripped the edge of my open locker door, keeping me upright. Corey and I had played together for almost ten years. I couldn't imagine going on a field without her.

"Maybe Parks & Rec this summer. I'll see," she said. "Not on the school team, though."

I wished I had time for a smoke, but everyone else was already in the gym.

"This year," she said, "I'm going out for track."

She did, too—ran the 880 and the mile. She was the best we had in her events, one of the three strongest performers on the girls' track team. We went to different practices; we rode different buses, played different schools. Once I went to a home meet on a Friday night, but Scott, Corey's boyfriend, was there and Corey didn't really talk to me. If she came to any of my softball games, I didn't know it.

Sometimes on my way to practice or a game, I would see Corey in the locker room, suiting up in her skimpy track shorts. I'd say, "Corey, what's up?" She'd say hi, but then some little sprinter or something would start chirping at her. I'd shoulder my bat and head outside, hiding my betrayal and outrage.

Practice for the Parks & Rec league started the week that school let out. We played at Stiles Field, named after the woman who started the Special Olympics in our town. There were actually four fields. A small playground by the parking lot accommodated brothers, sisters, sons and daughters dragged along to softball practice.

Corey was on the roster; I had already checked. Still, it was a relief to see her trot onto the field for our first practice. We threw the ball around a little bit, then lined up for batting practice.

Laura Jones, home for the summer from state college, said, "Hey chicks, what's up?"

"We did okay this year," I said. "Won all our games but two, no thanks to Corey."

Laura raised her eyebrows.

"She bailed on us," I said. "Ran track."

Corey didn't respond. Instead, she watched the playground, where two little boys whacked ardently at a tetherball. Corey and I used to swing over there, before we were big enough to play on a team.

"Really?" Laura asked.

Corey turned around. She picked up her bat, then asked Laura, "How about you? See much play this year?"

Laura shrugged; she was just a freshman. "I saw a lot," she said, "from the bench. It was fun, though." She was up then. We each would get five pitches, then rotate into the outfield.

"I got a job," I told Corey. "Landscape maintenance at Western Trails apartments."

"By the highway?" she asked. "That's where I run."

"That's a long way from where you live."

"Just over four miles," she said. Her bat hung loosely from her hand. She thumped the end of it into the dirt, then looked at me. "This summer I'm going to run one thousand miles."

I stared at Corey. When Corey showed up at practice I was

all set to forgive her lunacy of the spring, but this new plan sounded utterly insane.

On the playground, one of the tetherball boys yelled, "Yes! Yes! Yes!"

Corey watched Laura bat. "That's five," she said finally. "She got a piece of every one. You're up."

I stepped up to the plate, totally fanned the first pitch. The second ball thunked off the bottom of my bat, rolled weakly toward third base. "Linda—*focus*!" Corey yelled, and I hit a line drive clear into the next field.

We didn't get a chance to talk. A few days later, I was changing the spark plug on a lawn mower at Western Trails Apartments and spotted Corey coming down the road.

Her stride was beautiful, precise. Corey always had a clean style of running, but after track season it was totally pared down—a fluid roll of hips, legs stretching for pavement, hamstrings drawing her through the heel strike. Her head and shoulders were loose, but not slack, nothing extraneous; nothing that did not serve her single-minded forward progress.

Apparently she was serious about the thousand miles. Most mornings Corey passed the apartment complex between 8:00 and 9:00 a.m. Sometimes she waved; usually she just stared straight ahead. I'm not sure how she broke it down, but I know she often went ten to fifteen miles, day after day. After a few weeks, she grew gaunt and hard; her brown hair was always disheveled and sweaty, hanging in loose disturbed curls.

Every day it got a little hotter. I mowed grass, estimating the distance covered and quantifying the probable exertion. By afternoon I would put away a couple of quarts of Gatorade; I turned up each bottle and chugged it.

The more Corey ran, the skinnier she got. Of course you would expect that, and she was lean anyway, but at softball I noticed how her jersey began to hang on her. The veins had always stood out on the backs of her hands, ever since I met her, but now I could trace their course all the way up her forearm to her elbow. I found myself checking that, at practice and at games. I would look at her arms when she raised them over her head and stretched and see how prominent those veins had become.

As Corey became more insubstantial, she weighed heavily on my mind. It scared me and intrigued me. She seemed focused, serious; at the same time, she was hardly there. She stared into the distance as if her mind still raced along some dusty country road.

She began to suit up before coming to games; she never changed in the locker room at Stiles any more. Most of us did, even though the facilities were pretty gross, the lockers littered with gum wrappers and dead spiders curled up on their backs, floor sticky with old soda and beer. I started wanting to see Corey naked. Not the same way I wanted to see Miss Davis, the high-school librarian, naked—I never woke up in a sweat from a dream about Corey, never walked into a door because I was looking over my shoulder at her. It was just that somewhere in Corey there was something secret, some private thing that drove her down those gravel roads for ten, twelve, sometimes fifteen miles in a day.

In the dugout one Tuesday night in July, Corey reported her mileage: "I only ran five today, because of the game, then I went home and took a nap. Five miles today makes 448 total." Her brow creased. "That's a little under schedule; I've got not quite seven weeks left." Corey wrapped her arms around her stomach as she spoke, and clenched her right hand.

"You'll make it, if you really want it," I said. "You're past the blisters now. That slowed you down at first. You'll be able to increase as the summer goes on."

"I hope so." Corey stood and gripped a bat behind her neck. She was next up. She stretched back her elbows and twisted side to side, loosening up her waist. "I'm kind of worried about overuse injuries," she said. "Chondromalacia, or stress fracture, or even just shin splints." My passion had given us both a whole new vocabulary.

When Corey lowered the bat, one of her sleeves stayed caught on her skinny shoulder. A vein showed on the front of her biceps now. She was two weeks away from her eighteenth birthday; she shouldn't be that thin.

"Good nutrition helps keep up your energy," I said. "Maybe even supplements. You could ask one of the coaches. You been eating?"

She shrugged. "I don't get hungry. Haven't had breakfast since school let out. I drink a ton of water, but I just never feel all that much like eating."

She was up then, and got to second. I thought again of how the vein had showed on her upper arm. I decided to ask her if she wanted to go swimming—even if I didn't see her change, I'd have a better look at her.

The next day I went to the public library. I hadn't been in a long time; usually I checked out books from Miss Davis at school. The book-search program was new to me. It kicked out my request a couple of times, but I finally ended up with thirty-seven titles on eating disorders. I picked out two.

Checking them out made me feel conspicuous. The young guy behind the desk, probably a college student on summer break, kind of flicked his eyes over me as he scanned the books into the system.

One of the books said that anorexia nervosa is prevalent among females in the performing arts, particularly dancers. That might include athletes, too. The book gave a lot of signs, and some fit Corey, but I was just not sure.

The next morning I saw her striding down the highway. I thought of water, how it moved through her body, winding and compressing: driven through her heart, attending the muscles, smoothing joints, cushioning the 100,000 impacts of her daily course. I thought of cellular exchange, the escape of fluid through respiration and sweat. It made me thirsty. It made me want to jump into the river.

Corey said she would go swimming, but it would have to be in the evening. I asked if she wanted some beer. I thought she would say no, but she didn't so I got my cousin Joey to get me two six-packs. I had to give him four bottles, a hefty tariff.

I borrowed my dad's old pickup and drove to Corey's house. She was ready, sitting on the porch. As soon as we got down the road, we popped a beer apiece. I watched Corey to see if she was really drinking hers; sometimes anorexics give the appearance of eating or drinking, but really they are not consuming a substantial amount. She drank it, though, her fingers like bones wrapped around the brown glass.

We went to the old gravel quarry along the Meramec. When we were kids we rode our bikes out there and swam. It was usually deserted. The snakes creeped me out, but we didn't see them every time.

When we got to the bend of the river, I parked behind a pile of shiny tan river rock. Technically, it was private property, but the quarry had been defunct for decades.

Like me, Corey wore her swimsuit under a baggy T-shirt and shorts. She undressed on her side of the truck and dropped her clothes on the front seat. I did the same, then we anointed each other with Cutter repellent.

"You want the inner tubes?" I asked. We'd never been on the tubes at night. The river took a wide bend at the quarry, though, and there was little current because of the scooped-out depth.

"Sure," Corey said. She handed me the little compressor from the pickup bed and spread the flaccid tubes on the ground. We started another beer apiece, watching the swell of black rubber, then took beer and tubes to the bank. I handed my bottle to Corey; she held it until I was seated steady in the center of the tube, then handed me both bottles while she launched. I put them simultaneously to my mouth, acting silly, but spilled more than I swallowed. Corey paddled hard and retrieved her brew before I wasted any more.

After that we just floated, quiet. The moon came up right at sunset. It loomed so big that it looked like we could have paddled just a little more upstream and touched the cold blue surface of it.

Corey tipped her beer and drank. The bones of her shins looked sharp, as they did when she was twelve and growing tall. That year she was lanky, but still a little soft. Now she had become thin and anatomical, sinew and muscle and those blood vessels that stood out almost all the way up her arm. When she raised the bottle, a vein swelled in her shoulder.

In her swimsuit, though, I could see that Corey had a slight sag of belly. Not much, but as thin as the rest of her had become, it didn't look right. It made me think of those children of famine, malnourished and insectile, bloated thorax with spindly weakling limbs.

"You been eating, Corey?"

"You asked me that Tuesday," she said. "I don't eat breakfast. I like to run at eight, and I can't keep anything down if I run. Besides, I feel lighter if I don't eat."

"What about the rest of the day? You know you won't be able to keep running if you don't eat."

"I eat," she said. She polished off her beer. Took the bottle by the neck and aimed, sailed it low, end over end. It dropped with a soft clunk in the pile of loose gravel by the pickup.

Dark had settled. Corey scratched her upper arm and shivered. "I don't know about you, but I'm getting ate up."

"Yeah, me too. Let's get out."

We paddled our inner tubes to the bank and climbed out onto the coarse grass. Corey drained the melted ice from the cooler. I unscrewed the valve stems from the tubes, and we shared a beer as they flattened.

When I turned onto her street, Corey asked, "You want to come in for a while?"

"Sure." I wondered if she wanted me to spend the night. I hadn't done it in a long time. I pulled the truck into the driveway, well over to one side, and pushed in the creaky emergency brake.

Corey got out and almost fell. I don't know if she tripped or if her legs were just that sore. She had run 520 miles in the last six weeks, more than halfway to her goal.

She grinned, sheepish. "Must be the beer."

Her dad said "hi" without looking, and we went up to her room. Corey's hamstrings alternately bulged and grew taut all the way up the stairs. At the top she turned. "Are you looking at my ass?"

"You were limping," I said, but I could feel my face grow warm.

"Sometimes I'm pretty sore," she said.

"Christ, Corey, it's insane. A thousand miles over summer break. Why?"

She shrugged. "Why not? I know I can." She flopped down on her bed and eyed me. "What?"

My uncertainty must have showed, but I kept my voice firm. "I could massage your legs."

She looked dubious.

"I don't mind," I said. "If I'm going to be an exercise physiologist, I need to learn about the benefits of body work, especially in terms of performance enhancement."

"You didn't have nearly enough beer," Corey said, but she kicked off her shoes and rolled face-down on the bed.

The first touch was the hardest. In my palms I warmed some Jergens lotion, inhaling the faint almond smell, then stroked them up her left calf. The flesh was solid, pliable. Near the back of her knee I hit a mushy spot. "Shit," she hissed. She averted her head, facing the wall with the window. "No, go ahead. It feels good, really, but it's awfully sore there."

What I was feeling was not pain. Discomfort, certainly, at the way my senses sharpened when I touched her. Corey's tan skin felt luscious in my hands. I could smell her sweat, and a faint bitter hint of Cutter. I wanted to lean over and taste her back.

"Are you looking at my ass?"

"No!" I cast about. "I was looking at your prom picture." It was on the nightstand, by the bottle of Jergens: Corey and Scott, dressed in formals. I didn't go to prom. I didn't want to, and it was a good thing because nobody asked. Three of us from the softball team went to a movie, then sat by the river and got drunk. It was all right. We didn't have to dress up.

Corey had dumped Scott about the time school let out. She never said why. He was nice enough, I thought, but I never missed him. Corey never wanted to hang out when she and Scott were dating.

I finished kneading her hamstrings, mindful of the inner thigh, then lifted my hands. Corey rolled to her back and smiled, then closed her eyes and sort of extended her legs, offering them to me.

"How are your shins?" I asked.

"First two weeks they killed me," she said, "but now they're fine."

Lubricated with another handful of Jergens, I started from her feet. The massage just about put Corey to sleep. Not me; I was thoroughly disturbed. I worked up her shin and into the quads.

I had never had my hands on a woman before—not like this. Corey maybe wasn't quite a woman, but she was surely no kid.

The pit of my stomach burned, a hot yearning overlaid by crawling fear. It felt awful, but the yearning flared and spread, and it was kind of wonderful. A cold knot stayed in my stomach, and the yearning traveled north and south. A piece of it lodged in my chest, tender, welcoming; the other part went straight to my groin and started a rock'n'roll band.

I finished up, shaken. Corey stretched and groaned like an old dog. "Thanks, Linda," she said. "That was great."

She was apparently not going to move, so I dragged the rolled sleeping bag from her closet floor, then got a pillow and top sheet from the hall closet. A shower would have been nice—river water and sweat had left me sticky, and my hair was stiff from silt. I felt a little sticky in the crotch, as well. But Corey's jaw had loosened; her breath was deep and slow. I snapped off the light, spread the sleeping bag on the floor next to her bed.

The gripping lust had faded, but that unexpected tenderness still lodged in my heart. It made me want to touch Corey, not to arouse her, but just to pet her like I would my cat. It troubled me.

The flesh of her legs had been more substantial than I expected. They were thin; unlike her upper body, though, some muscle bulk remained.

Her face had looked almost skeletal when I first turned off the light, an assembly of shadows, edged too sharply by the light that straggled through the window. *Christ, Corey, doesn't anybody look at you but me?* The veins stood out on her hands and arms; even in sleep the blood ran close to the surface. Corey was much too thin.

Except for her stomach. That slight curve of belly surprised me. It didn't seem consistent with anorexia; the eating disorders books said that anorexics develop a scaphoid abdomen. I had to look it up; it means curved in, like a crescent.

Maybe she *was* getting malnutrition, like those pictures of starving children. "Corey?"

She grunted, stirred a little.

"I know I keep asking you this, but are you eating?"

Corey cleared her throat and rolled to her side. "I told you—yes. I don't feel like eating in the morning, because of the run. Sometimes I eat a little when I get back. Usually I'm too hot. I eat lunch, though, and dinner. Snacks." She laughed. "Beer. Don't worry so much."

"It's just—you've gotten so skinny. I checked out a book about eating disorders, and the signs all seem to fit."

"Oh, for the love of God." Corey rolled to her back, hands behind her head. "Linda, I don't have an eating disorder. I just want to run. You try running a thousand miles over a summer and see what it does to *your* body."

Cheap shot—*ten* thousand miles probably wouldn't make me skinny. If Corey was a greyhound, I was more of a beagle. "Maybe I worry too much," I said. "It just scares me, Corey. You've never looked like this. And anorexia—it's nothing to fool around with. Sometimes people die. You grow weird body hair. The calcium comes out of your bones. You could get stress fractures. It messes up your organs—your periods stop."

"Already did," Corey said. She lay absolutely still, staring at the ceiling.

"Oh, Corey, you've got to get some help. We need to—"

"In May," she said softly. "Around the middle of May."

"But you didn't start running until school was out. It had to have been sometime..." My voice trailed off and I went cold all over.

"That was June," she said. "I started running the first week of June, and I'm going to keep running until I hit a thousand miles, and if my period has not come back by then, I'll just run until it does."

I sat up, gripped my knees and pulled them tight to my chest. I was panting, almost gasping for air. The picture of Corey and Scott caught my eye; in the dark bedroom it was a black rectangle, the glass distorting light, rejecting it, and the picture empty behind it.

You don't have to do this, I wanted to say. *Come with me—let's go somewhere, someplace people don't know us. I'll get a job, I'll help you. I don't care if I become an exercise physiologist. It can wait.*

Corey lay there silent, her blood ever closer to the surface. She lay there waiting for a piece of herself to die. I wanted to stop her, to save her. The yearning in my chest pulsed hotly as a torn artery, and I felt like I might suffocate. *If you had been with me, this never would have happened. You and Scott—if you had been with me—*

Seventeen and helpless, reeling with despair, I fell back on the sleeping bag.

"You can't tell anyone," Corey said. "No one." The sheets rustled and her hand appeared over the side of the mattress, reaching.

I took it and held it, held it a long time, my forearm propped against the bed rail and box spring. I thought her arm would go numb, and maybe it did, but she held on until I fell asleep.

When I woke in the morning, Corey was pulling on her running shoes. "Hey, champ," she said. "It's going to be hot today. I'm starting early." Then she left. In the still house, her feet rattled down the stairs. She closed the front door gently. I strained to hear the rhythm of her sneakers on the road. Too soon, it was gone. I rolled the sleeping bag and stowed it in the closet.

By mid-August, Corey had over nine hundred miles behind her. Gaunt, driven, she ran past the apartment complex almost every morning, now going eight miles out and eight miles back. She still came to the games, still reported her mileage, but anyone could see her mind was not on softball. She hardly spoke at all.

There came a day I didn't see her run, a Tuesday. She wasn't at the game that night, and when she hadn't passed the apartments by Thursday morning, I called her on my lunch break.

She said come over after work, that she would be at home. When I got there, two of the younger kids were playing in the yard, running through a sprinkler, and the long brown legs of her sister Irene reminded me so much of Corey at that age. Her brother George opened the door for me. "She's in her room," he said.

The door was open just a crack, and Corey was on the bed. "Come in," she said.

I did, and closed the door. She scooted toward the window, and I sat cross-legged by her feet. "I haven't seen you in a couple days."

"I've only got twenty-three miles to go," she said. "I'm taking a break; I can knock that out in two days. One, if I have to."

I nodded. Corey was pale, and her face looked different. Less strained, not so stern. She kind of looked slack. "It came," she said.

I couldn't think of anything to say. Nothing. That feeling welled up in my chest again, and I gritted my teeth until it stopped.

"I need to get out of here," Corey said. "You want to get a Coke or something?"

"Sure," I said. I drove us to McDonald's. We talked about senior year, the classes we would have. Corey said she might go out for cross-country. "Might as well," I said.

That summer, before our senior year, Corey ran one thousand miles. She finished the last ten the day before school started.

In the fall, she ran cross-country. That must have felt like a vacation; she took third in state. By spring, she was seeing a guy at the junior college, and not into training so much.

She played on the softball team senior year, and we had a hell of a season. Everyone was glad to have Corey back. I never said a thing, and I don't guess anyone else ever knew.

One thing changed, though—Corey's eyes. At softball, in class, even driving to the river with a beer between her thighs, her eyes were focused beyond the horizon. I was Corey's closest friend, but a thousand miles remained between us.

Bios

Tracy L. Barnett is an independent writer and photographer focused on sustainability, indigenous rights and travel. She has served as an editor and staff writer at the *San Antonio Express-News*, the *Houston Chronicle* and *Intercontinental Cry*, among others. Her work has appeared in the *Washington Post, BBC Travel, National Geographic Traveler en Español, Esquire Latin America* and many more. She is currently at work on a book about her 2010 backpacking trip through Latin America: *Looking for Esperanza: One woman's search for hope through the Other America*. You can follow her travels and ruminations at www.tracybarnettonline.com.

Nathan Boone, a native of Peculiar, Missouri by way of LaCygne, Kansas, is a blue collar writer whose work tends to reflect his working-class origins. He currently resides in Columbia, Missouri with his wife and their five dogs.

John Brown is an environmental expert witness, retired in 2015, with plenty of stories to tell. Enjoys poetry and songwriting as well as working on short stories and a current novel related to a haunted church. Masters from Texas A&M University, PhD. from North Carolina State and Post Doc from Duke University in 1988. Resides in Boonville, MO along the Missouri River.

Carol Gorski Buckels writes poetry in DeLand, Florida, which is more similar to the Ozarks than you might expect. For a period of time, her husband Steve's family lived on a farm in the Ozarks, where they raised hogs on a rocky hillside overlooking the Niangua River.

Bridget Bufford leads weekly creative writing workshops. Participants write from prompts, read aloud and give feedback. Critique is available for work in revision. Find out more at www.bridgetbufford.com. Her novel *Cemetery Bird* was nominated for a Pushcart Prize, and *Minus One: A Twelve-Step Journey* was short-listed for a Lambda Literary Award. Shorter works have appeared in several fat anthologies and thin litmags.

Kathleen Cain lives on the edge of the Ozarks in Columbia, MO. She takes daily walks in the wooded park near her home, cherishing the solitude, beauty and changing seasons. Writing has been a pastime of hers for many years, often as a meditation on nature.

Jim Coffman is a retired minister with 40 years active service. His poetry collections *Gravel Dust and Dreams* and the sequel *Outside the Crowd* were published by Pudding House Publications. Jim is a member of the Missouri Writers' Guild and the CCMWG.

Marta Ferguson is the co-editor of *Drawn to Marvel: Poems from the Comic Books* (Minor Arcana Press, 2014) and the author of *Mustang Sally Pays Her Debt to Wilson Pickett* (Main Street Rag, 2005). She is the sole proprietor of Wordhound Writing & Editing Services, LLC (http://www.wordhound.com).

Ida Bettis Fogle lives in Columbia with a houseful of food critics. Her poetry, short fiction and creative nonfiction have appeared in various publications, including *Well Versed*, *Thema* and the anthology *Uncertain Promise.*

Steve Gallagher spends his precious time researching 19th-century central Missouri, climbing the Missouri river hills, and trying to impress writing group members with his compositions. Moreover, he spins records which were made in the first four decades of the 20th century, at KOPN, a community radio station in Columbia, Missouri (which also streams live online).

Julie Gardner writes and leads writing groups in Seattle, WA. She and John have been married 40 years. They no longer smoke, but still tip, howl, and love—mostly joyfully.

Rebecca Graves has published several articles and book chapters in the world of academia where she works by day as a medical librarian. In her off hours, she writes in the genres of fiction and poetry. She lives in Columbia with the inventor and jazz musician Pack Matthews.

Emme Hanson drew much inspiration and encouragement from her years participating in Creative Writing of Columbia. She has done her best to recreate the experience since moving away, participating in multiple writing groups and convincing fellow writers of the value of an hour of quiet communal writing.

Von Pittman grew up in a Navy family. He has worked as a sales clerk, a proctor, a shipboard engineer, a garbage man, and university flunkey. He has published fiction in *The First Line, Cantos, Cuivre River Review, Perspectives Magazine, Crime and Suspense, Well Versed*, and a number of local and regional anthologies.

Sady Mayer Strand is the Director of the Student Success Center at Stephens College and a member of Women Who Submit, an organization encouraging women in the publication process. Strand has long been under the spell of the Ozarks--especially the region's timeworn mountains, expressive vernacular, and enduring ballads.

Emily McBride Theroff was born and raised in the Ozarks; she now lives in Columbia, Missouri. She works as a mental health professional and writes fiction and non-fiction. She was published in *Interpretations II*, *Interpretations III*, and *Solstice: a winter anthology*.

CPSIA information can be obtained
at www.ICGtesting.com
Printed in the USA
FSOW01n0604210117
29897FS